The Memoirs Of
Man

2

The Memoirs Of A Very Fortunate Man

Written By

Captain John Cyril Bennett
Royal Welch Fusiliers

This is a moving personal account of a Welsh lad's journey to the battlefields of France and Asia with the British armed forces. It is simply retold with an honesty and integrity which serves as a tribute to the friends that become lost along the way. It is also in parts humorous, tragic, compelling and inspirational.

The book ends with gratitude to the 'Heroes Return' scheme which allowed the author to revisit Kohima in Burma where he was in battle with the Japanese, and to say farewell to his fallen friends and comrades.

Rock Road Books Ltd
Royston
Hertfordshire
England

SBN   0955210305
9 780955 210303

INTRODUCTION

For the last twenty years, I have lived in the small market town of Great Dunmow in the heart of the county of Essex. My wife Margaret and I had retired from teaching in Chelmsford, some 10 miles east of where we lived, and in a very short time, we were involved in a number of community activities in Dunmow. I was introduced to the "Dunmow Club" by my son John.

The club had been formed by a member of the Faulkes family of Great Dunmow, in honour of the men of Dunmow who had left the village to fight in the 1914 – 1918 war. In addition to forming the club, a house in the High Street, now called "The Hazels", and the surrounding grounds were donated to it for its headquarters. From 1918 at its inception until the beginning of the year 2005 it has remained a "men's club". There are no lady members but on special occasions ladies may attend club functions accompanied by a club member. Soon after I joined the club I became a member of a very select group of men who had retired at 65 years of age and who sat in an area that was jokingly called "Death Row" by the younger members. About 1990 we changed the name to "The Departure Lounge", a much preferred and less depressing expression!

Over a pint, I have listened to stories and tales recounted by retired farm workers, the local doctor, ex-wartime servicemen, tradesmen and others who represent all walks of life. Some of the stories were, and still are, hilarious, others very sad. Having listened to so many of these over the years, I one day realised that not one of them had ever been committed to paper, a great pity as they risk being lost in the mists of time.

Unfortunately too, the numbers in the departure lounge have declined over the years and those gone been replaced with new, younger faces. Those who have gone have taken their anecdotes with them.

After some encouragement from my three children, I decided that, yes it would be a good thing to write about my own experiences in the hope that in years to come, someone might find them interesting. I have lived through an age that has probably seen more change than any other age in history and I hope my efforts will be of interest to some of you.

If at some time, for whatever reason, someone tells me to go to hell, I can honestly say that I really don't care two hoots. I have been there a few times but always returned.

A Brief Urdu Glossary

British troops who had dealings with the Indian people needed to know a basic set of Urdu vocabulary. Some basic words are listed below:	
Acha	Good
Asti	Slowly
Badmash	Undesirable
Bahut	Very
Baksheesh	Tips or alms
Bas	Enough
Basha	Hut
Bhisti	Water carrier
Bibi	Girl
Burra	Big
Chaggal	Canvas water bag
Chapal	Sandals
Char	Tea
Charbash	Well done
Chapoy	Rope bed
Chatti	Earthenware jug
Chaung	Dry river bed
Chota	Small
Coggage	Paper

Dacoit	Robber
Dafta	Office
Dekko	Look
Dhobi	Laundry
Durri	Rough woven rug
Eepyippi	Army tent
Ek	One
Hoqiya	Finish
Idhar-ao	Come here
Jao	Go
Jildi	Quickly
Karo	Do
Khua	Hillside
Kiswaste	Why
Kya	What
Lathi	Stave or stick
Maidan	Open ground
Mallum	Understand
Mukkin	Butter
Nappi	Barber
Nichi	Underneath
Pani	Water
Pialla	Mug

Pice	Small coin
Puggle pani	Booze
Pukka	Genuine
Sahib	Sir or master
Salaams	Greetings
Sepoy	Soldier
Shikars	Hunter
Susti	Lazy
Tiffin	Midday meal
Tonga	One-horse cart
Uppe	Above
Wallah	servant

CHAPTER ONE

Family Life in Wales

When I look back at my childhood, I see happiness, warmth, laughter and lots and lots of love. In my minds eye, I don't see my brother Roy, or my sister Beryl who came along later. However, I remember my grandmother who was blessed with both a large bosom and an enormous lap, a cheerful lady who made wonderful things to eat. She had a large cupboard which, when the doors were opened, gave out the beautiful aroma of herbs and spices.

My grandfather had a big moustache which curled up at the ends, and he smoked a pipe. Tommy was their son, Enid and Anita their daughters. Tommy, or Uncle Tom, worked as a chemist in the now disappeared Risca steel works in South Wales. Aunt Nita was married to a Trades' Union official who worked in a colliery in Crosskeys and Enid, my mother, was married to Thomas Samuel Bennett who was in charge of the Accounts Department of Mynnyd Islywn District Council.

My father, mother and I first lived at 21 Dany Graig Road, Risca and later at No. 7 Brynteg Avenue, Pontllanfraith, Monmouthshire. On many occasions, we would all gather at Gran's house for musical evenings where my mother played the piano to accompany singers and instrumentalists. My father was a tenor and he with Aunt Nita, who had a beautiful soprano voice, often sang duets together.

On such evenings, I rarely stayed awake for the whole duration and would be put to bed. It was always a lovely surprise to wake up and find Uncle Tommy, who was my hero, snoring peacefully on his side of the bed. He took me everywhere, fishing, the Whitsun Fair, even on his motor bike. I learned later that Gran (Eliza Davies) owned her own bread, cake and pastry shop (hence the 'wonderful things to eat' I suppose) and that Gramps had helped build the first railway through the Congo in Africa. He often suffered relapses of malaria and kept a bottle of quinine by his bedside. He (John Davies) had the first private car in the Pontynister part of Risca and owned his own, plus two or three other houses in Wyndham Terrace down near the canal in the town.

Thomas Bennett, my father was born in Risca and after leaving Risca Grammar School worked as a checkwayman in a colliery, recording the amount and quality of the coal produced. Before the 1914-18 war he emigrated to Canada and worked as a butcher in Montreal. When war was declared against Germany he joined a Canadian cavalry regiment and was trained as a signaller. Heliography was in its infancy and he was trained in the use of lights, mirrors, the sun, flag signalling and Morse Code. On arriving in England with his regiment he requested and was granted a transfer to the British Army. He took part in the Battle for the Somme and was later wounded in the neck at Mons. After the war, he returned to Risca where his father and mother lived in Danycraig Road. Both his mother and father were staunch teetotallers and tried to persuade him to be one also. I never saw him the worse for drink but he enjoyed the company of other men and a glass of beer. As a result, when my grandparents died, they cut him out of their wills.

Thomas Samuel Bennett was very popular – as a young man, he played rugby for Wales. He spoke fluent French and was a mathematician. As a father, he was kindly and just and never raised his hand in anger.

Enid May Bennett (nee Davies) my mother was nursing at a hospital in London when I was born. As my father was at war, she returned to her parents in Risca. I arrived on 10th June 1916. She was a brilliant pianist and was an accompanist for many Welsh singers who sang at eisteddfods and concerts. She was also an accomplished elocutionist and won two chairs for elocution at the Welsh National Eisteddfod. She was a very warm gentle person who could play the classics without music but could not count up her grocery bill mentally without the help of her fingers

My brother Roy, born on 21st January 1919, was a dreamer. He would sit for hours reading "A Child's Garden Of Verse" or play with a couple of ladybirds in a matchbox, the world just passed him by. I was his idol and he loved to be with me. When I was soldiering in England, he would go to great lengths to visit me and perhaps stay for a few days in a nearby village. He served in Egypt during the second world war and towards the end of the war was granted ten days leave of absence in order to get married. His fiancée was a young lady called May who taught German and French at a grammar school in Brecon. Roy and May both belonged to a tennis club in Pontllanfraith. They partnered one another and before Roy was posted to Egypt they became engaged to be married. I was best man and my wife Margaret attended the wedding service with me. The ceremony took place in the Wesleyan Chapel in Pontllanfraith, Monmouthshire. After the wedding, Margaret and I stayed for a snack but had to leave early as I was needed back on duty at the barracks in Newtown, mid-Wales.

The following day I received a telephone call from my father telling me that May had been feeling unwell after we had left. My mother had called out our own doctor to her and he had arranged for May to be taken to hospital. I was very surprised to learn that the hospital was in Abergavenny and was a mental institution.

A few days later, I accompanied Roy to the hospital and on our arrival, a nursing orderly suggested that Roy wait in the office whilst I went to see May. This we agreed to do and out I went with the orderly. When I saw May, I immediately realised why Roy had been told to wait. It was explained that all her front teeth had been extracted because she had been biting her lips and arms and that she was demented. She had lost a lot of weight and looked dreadful. Worst of all I was told that she hadn't long to live as she was rotten with tuberculosis.

I persuaded Roy that he should not see May as she was. He reluctantly agreed and we returned home. We were informed a few days later that May had died. We learned too that all her family had a history of tuberculosis and that her father and brother had also died of it. The marriage was never consummated.

My sister Beryl, was born 4th September 1921. From the day of the baby's birth, Roy and I were encouraged to hold and care for her, we enjoyed every minute of it and the three of us grew up in a very happy relationship. We went to a school named 'Libanus' which was located between Pontllanfraith and Blackwood. Unlike schools of today where schools change staff quite frequently, the Libanus staff stayed the same, Mrs Rees from the local farm was head of the infants school, whilst Mr. Groves and Mr. Coleman were teachers in the senior school. Mr. Ray Coleman remained a personal friend of mine until his death in 1951.

Apart from Christmas and New Year, there were three occasions in the year which we all looked forward to. One was the Whitsun Fair at Risca. The others were the Church Parade and the Blackwood Agricultural Show. The Whitsunday activities were to held to celebrate the resurrection of Christ and were usually accompanied by a feast.

The Church Parades were made at Whitsuntide when it was very hot and the tar on the roads would melt. We used to march a distance of about three miles singing and carrying the church banner in front of us. On arrival at the church, we had sandwiches and seedcake, trifle and soft drinks. The following day it was sports day on the sports field when we competed for prizes like penknives, torches and other similar 'must have' trivia. Such fun times.

The Risca Fair was enormous. There were coconut shies, roundabouts, chair-a-planes, darts games, and sideshows where we fished for goldfish. There was also a boxing booth where people like Tommy Farr would offer to fight three rounds with anyone brave enough to try.

We usually returned home carrying one or two coconuts and goldfish that would last about two days, defeated very quickly by the loving and constant attention of three small children with six sticky hands. They were happy times. Some years later at the fair, I boxed three rounds with a coloured boy, Bill Bailey, who lived in a hillside cottage on the Graig in Risca. We were paid five shillings each.

It was about this time that I found my first girlfriend. Her name was Gwen Cole and she played the organ in church when the official organist could not attend. We sometimes arranged to attend well before the service started and she played dance tunes on the organ. She was a good sport and we went to the cinema together and later on to the Friday night dancing lessons at the nineties Welfare Institute in Blackwood.

When I was sixteen I joined the army and left home. We wrote to one another for a while and when I went on leave we met and continued seeing one another. Rugby, boxing and studies combined with military duties took up more and more of my time and we stopped writing. When I was about 22 and on leave I met her again and was introduced to her fiancé. I didn't see Gwen again until 1944 when Margaret and I were married. Gwen played the organ at our wedding and by this time was happily married herself and had a two year old son.

During the summer holiday when the schools were closed, the Bedwelty Agricultural Show used to take place on the Blackwood showground. It always seemed to be a beautiful day. One show, I spent the morning of the show sitting on the farm fence next to the railway sidings in Pontllanfraith. It was there that most of the bigger animals arrived for the show. There were horses for the trots, Suffolk Punches with their manes plaited and tails be-ribboned, bulls with rings in their noses and as one train unloaded and moved away, another would arrive to take its place. It was wonderful. In the afternoon, I went to the show ground and sold program booklets, these were a shilling each. For every ten I sold, I received one shilling and had a good day, plus free entry to the marquees and other interesting places.

Later that year as autumn and winter were on the way, Mum bought Beryl a pair of tall button-up leather boots which had to be fastened using a button hook. She hated these boots and Roy and I would tease her about them. Beryl then decided as a result of all this that she would run away from home and go to the local lodging house where the tramps and ne'er-do-wells were taken in for the night. The place was called 'Pratts'.

She packed her little case with things she needed and headed for the lodging house. We followed her trying not to be seen and we found that the nearer she got to the house, the slower she became until she stopped altogether at the entrance to the narrow lane which led to the house. It was then that we rescued her from a 'fate worse than death'. We often have a laugh about that now.

Then came a worrying period. One day Beryl was well, the next vomiting and unable to eat, even what she drank came back up. Mum, who was a district nurse, called in our doctor, a Dr. Mackay, who came a number of times to see her. But she grew progressively weaker and weaker.

My father also did the accounts for a local herbalist, a Mr. Griffiths and he asked him if he would come and see

Beryl. After his visit Dad went with him and brought back a bottle of his medicine. Beryl was given one dose and immediately spat out a lump of black toffee (known locally as Blackjack) which had been lodged in the back of her throat. After that, we had a totally new outlook on herbalism.

I missed a great deal of Beryl's and Roy's formative years because I joined the army in 1933 at the age of 16 and only saw them when I went on leave. I wrote home regularly and kept them up to date with what I was doing and my father did the same for me. Beryl passed her eleven plus exam and followed me on to the grammar school. Roy, sadly, did not do so well and went to the local secondary school.

My last teacher at Libanus school was, as already mentioned, Mr. Coleman. He had been in the navy during the Great War and had trained as a teacher afterwards. He never shouted in the classroom, we all worked hard and his kindly manner rubbed off on us all. Many of the children belonged to poor mining families and he often sent me to get milk and bread for those who had had little to eat before coming to school.

Whilst in his class, the time came for me to sit the eleven plus exam. I was told to ask my parents to send in my birth certificate for registration purposes and this was duly given to me at home in a sealed brown envelope one evening for the next day at school. I took this along to the head teacher the following morning and then the next day, having been checked and recorded, it was returned to me to take home.

On the way home, I realised that the envelope was opened and I decided to look at the paper inside. To my great surprise, I found that I was not John Cyril Bennett but that I had been christened Cyril John Hutchinson and that my father had been a merchant banker and living in Regents Park, London. Thinking about this as I made my way home, I decided that Thomas Samuel Bennett had been a very good father to me and that that was enough. I sealed the envelope and returned it to my parents without letting them know I had read it. September 1928.

I was fortunate to have passed the eleven plus and was luckier still to receive a place at the Pontllanfraith Grammar School. My new school was just across the road from where I lived in Brynteg Avenue. On the school badge was the motto "Cais Loywach Nen", Welsh for 'Seek Fairer Skies'.

Mr. David Bowen was headmaster, a keen disciplinarian, pretty handy with the cane which he concealed in the folds of his gown. At that time, only soccer was played at the school but rugby football was introduced that year and Mr. Gordon Jones, the maths teacher, was trainer and organiser. He was a good teacher well liked by pupils and staff. He later taught Beryl and her friend Margaret Evans who in 1944 became my wife. Margaret's brother Douglas and her sisters Beatrice and Joan were also educated at this school.

Later, Beryl trained as a teacher in Crewe, Margaret and Beatrice trained as teachers in Swansea, I trained at Shenstone Training College For Teachers near Leominster in Staffordshire and at London University. Douglas became an electrical engineer with the South

17

Wales Coal Board. After a period at university, Joan married a barrister who became a judge and who is now Lord Justice Ackner and a member of the House of Lords.

My schooling became periods of learning between and interfering with games of rugby or cricket and by the end of 1932, I had the necessary qualifications to apply for teacher training. About two years previously, I had tonsillitis so badly that they had to be lanced – I was off school for about a month. This set me back, particularly with my maths and, to catch up, my father sat with me in the evenings. One of these evenings, after finishing extra homework, my mother asked me to go and shop for her. She gave me the necessary money and instead of shopping, I caught a bus to Pontypridd. From there I walked along country lanes to where my grandfather kept a pub. My gran had died when I was about nine years old and 'Gramps' had sold his houses in Risca and remarried a lady who was not liked by the family.

It was quite scary walking in the dark with owls hooting and only the occasional car passing by. Eventually, I came to the pub and went in to meet my grandfather and his lady. They made a fuss of me and like sensible people, without telling me they phoned my parents to tell them I was ok. Why I ever did that, I will never know. Was I rebelling as a teenager or were my hormones working overtime? When I went home after a few days, my father opened the door and said "Hello Son, your Mum and Bel and Roy are waiting for you inside". Coming home was wonderful and I knew I would never willingly do anything like that again.

2 January 1933

My father was in the bathroom shaving and I went in to clean my teeth. He asked me what my intentions were for the future –was I going to train as a teacher or had I any other ideas?

I had a friend named Reggie Webb who had gone to the local senior school, had worked in the local grocers after leaving school at 15, and had joined the army. He described the training he did, the sports and games which were available to him, and in general, his view of life as a soldier.

I had already given this a lot of thought and as I had already learned a lot from my mother, the district nurse, I said to my father – "I would like to join the army Medical Corps". He was quiet for a few seconds and then replied "If that is what you wish to do, then you can do it". The following day he gave me enough money to travel to Newport and to keep me going for a few days.

CHAPTER TWO

Joining Up

The recruiting officer was at the Cavalry Barracks in Newport and that's where I eventually ended up. Having reported to him, I was placed with another young person in an office where we were firstly questioned and then made to complete the necessary papers. There followed an arithmetic test which was the equivalent of a ten year old's paper for junior pupils, followed by an English junior paper. I finished both in about 15 minutes and later was given English and Maths papers for seniors. These were completed in about half an hour.

The young man with me was from Chepstow, his surname was Dickenson. He was sent home to collect his birth certificate to prove that he was eighteen years of age. I was sweating because I was only sixteen, coming up for seventeen the June approaching. But I wasn't sent home, for some reason they accepted my word.

Later that day, Dickenson came back with his certificate and we were both taken to an upstairs room which was above the stables of the cavalry horses. It was a dreadful night, the horses behaved as horses do, they neighed and blew through their nostrils, broke wind and rattled chains, then, after the longest night of my life, the soldiers came in at dawn to feed and clean them.

That morning after we had washed and had breakfast, we were taken to the office where I was told that I could not join the Medical Corps as there were no vacancies. I was very disappointed but felt that having got this far, I had to join something. So I asked the officer "Then where are the vacancies?". His reply was that there were vacancies with the Royal Welch Fusiliers which prompted me to ask what they did. "They are a very famous infantry regiment and their training depot is at Wrexham in North Wales" was the reply.

I had a rough idea where Wrexham was because of their soccer team. I didn't want to show my ignorance however, by asking what infantry were so I looked questioningly at Dickenson who then asked me "So shall we give it a try?". I agreed that we should. We then had to repeat the Oath Of Allegiance to the Crown, were paid two shillings and told to go home and tell our parents, and report back the following day to collect our railway passes to Wrexham.

That evening, I neglected to tell my parents that I was no longer planning to be a medical orderly, only that I was going off to Wrexham for training. I reported back to the recruiting officer along with Dickenson and we were then taken to Newport station where we were despatched to the Wrexham barracks. 3rd January 1933, we were met at the station by a very smart corporal who introduced himself as Corporal Thomas and "not to be called Sir!". When addressed, we were to respond "Yes, Corporal" or "No, Corporal" and that was it.

On arrival at the actual barracks, the first person we encountered was the sentry, dressed in khaki, gleaming black boots, white webbing belt and carrying a rifle with bayonet fixed. We didn't go in through the main gate that he was guarding but through a side gate nearby. I was beginning to realise just then, having seen the sentry, what an infantryman did.

The next few days were magic, there was shower time, haircut - short back and sides, introduction to about twenty other recruits, medical inspection and the dreaded inoculations. The dread may have been inspired by the sight of a medical orderly sharpening a needle on the side of a Swan Vesta matchbox!!

Then came Sergeant Roberts and Lance Corporal Chester and we quickly transformed from a disorganised rabble into "C Squad", January 1933. In the beginning, there were young men who were born and brought up in North Wales and who spoke very little English, those who could not march swinging the left arm with the left leg, some who didn't know their left from their right and so on but in six months they would not have been recognised as the rabble they had been. Sergeant Roberts, Corporal Thomas and Lance Corporal (Doc.) Chester, as he came to be known from the number of blisters he burst, had done an excellent job on us all.

Recently, March 2002, I have seen a film in TV depicting the training of soldiers for the 1939 war and heard the filthy and demeaning language supposedly used by the instructors to their trainee soldiers. It may have happened then but in 1933 the three instructors were gentlemen and I have heard men chastised verbally for poor drill etc. but never sworn at.

Life became disciplined and orderly. We were awakened by a bugler who played 'Reveille' at 6.30am. Between then and 8.00am, beds and blankets were folded neatly, barrack room chores were completed, every man had a job to do, dusting and cleaning, buffing the floor, cleaning washbasins and taps in the washroom.

Following this came personal hygiene, washing and shaving and preparing for parade and inspection at 9.00am. Breakfast was between 8.00 and 8.30am followed by half an hour for toileting and dressing for the parade. Every man had to be on the parade ground at least two minutes before the 'Fall In' order was given.

The initial inspection was carried out by the sergeant with the corporal and lance corporal in attendance. When they were satisfied, we were marched off to the centre of the 'square', as the parade ground was called, and lined up in two lines for inspection by the Orderly Officer for the day.

If the O.O. complained about anything to a man, "hair too long", "belt not blancoed (whitened) properly", "cap badge not sufficiently polished" and so on, then these things had to be rectified by the following day or else it meant "Jankers" – extra work fatigues and no passes out of camp or barracks. The only part of our training which I didn't particularly like, which we took part in during the spring and summer months, was the Saturday cross country run. It took place in all weathers and the course was about five miles long. On the north side of the barracks, the ground fell away through scrubland to the river Clywedog which was crossed by a small footbridge. The course went over the bridge and turned right towards Wrexham following the footpath near the river for about two miles. It then recrossed the river, turned right again and back along the other side to return to the barracks.

After the very first run, I was a long way behind the front runners and when I got back, the showers were running cold. I decided that on the next run I would cross the river about half way around the course and join the front runners along the return stretch. I followed my plan and when I got down into the water, was delighted to find that it was shallow enough to wade across without having to swim. I waded through and then clambered up the opposite bank on to the towpath and straight into the arms of Sergeant Roberts. I was ordered around the full course again, along with some half dozen others who had also tried to beat the system, once again we had cold showers. There was no reprimand, we had suffered enough.

About three quarters of our training had passed and I had been 'caught' by Doc. Chester when he walked into the barrack room and asked "can anyone here ride a bike?". I raised my hand and said a firm "Yes Corporal" and Doc. asked me to follow him. We went down the stairs where I was given a bucket and mop and told to clean the concrete steps. He said "let that be a lesson to you , my lad, never volunteer for anything". A lesson well learnt.

At about this time, I started taking my first class certificate in mathematics at evening class and was promoted to squad lance corporal. Corporals Thomas and Doc. Showed me how to make out duty rosters for guard duty and fatigue groups where certain misdemeanours had been committed and which had attracted extra chores – potato and vegetable cleaning, washing plates and dishes after meals, general labour in the kitchen – all favourites which had to be done in free time.

The acquisition of my first stripe gave me an extra thee pence a day pay. I was now 17 years old and on two shillings and three pence pay per day. I didn't smoke or drink alcohol at that time and I made an allotment of five shillings each week to my father who saved it for me. When the six months of training were complete, we were given ten days leave with pay. I went home in uniform carrying my kitbag which held all my worldly possessions.

Before setting out for home, I creased my trousers, cleaned up buttons and cap badge, blancoed my webbing belt, polished my chinstrap and, most importantly of all, pressed the five black ribbons which adorned my collar and lay down my back. The ribbons, which only the Royal Welch Fusiliers were entitled to wear, were called a 'Flash' and originated from the time when soldiers in the British army wore red coats and a 'Queue' which held the tarred pigtails of their hair. The hair was tarred to stop head lice and was said to have been "at many a siege and sack and pointed a moral and adorned the back." I was very proud of it.

The Author, Wrexham Barracks, N. Wales

1933, aged 17

CHAPTER THREE

1st Battalion Royal Welch Fusiliers, Twenty Third Of Foot

Early in July 1933, I travelled to Tidworth which was a garrison town in Hampshire, and reported to the Orderly Room, "4189836, Lance Corporal John Cyril Bennett". Before the first week was out, I had, when not on duty, been dubbed "Blondie Bennett" from my fair hair. I had now become a real member of the First Battalion Royal Welch Fusiliers 23rd Of Foot in the British Army.

The battalion was led by a colonel with about twenty eight subordinate officers of various ranks, a regimental sergeant major, four company sergeant majors and six hundred men made up of sergeants, corporals, lance corporals and fusiliers (private soldiers).

The regimental sergeant major was the man responsible for the quality of drill and discipline in the regiment, he was revered by most, even the younger officers, and some were truly scared of him. After a few years, I came to understand what an enormous task he had and how efficient a man he was. He, like many of the officers and men, wore medals from the 1914 -18 war.

I took to this life like a duck to water, I was in charge of a barrack room with a mixture of men, a few like myself and others seasoned soldiers who had spent time in India and other parts of the world which were at that time parts of the British Empire.

Every day was a new experience, I applied for and was granted, two hours a week at the army school to take maths, map reading and geography. I attended classes with junior officers and NCOs on many subjects allied to soldiering including Camouflage and Concealment. I took a Sniper's Course on rifle shooting and was awarded a further pay increase and Sharpshooter's badge for my sleeve.

The teacher taking the mathematics course was from my own home town. He had been to grammar school in Pengam and then after university had joined the Army Education Corps. His sister had been at my own school. Although I knew this, I don't thinks he was aware of it. His name was Gibbons. At the end of 1933, I had passed the following with distinctions in most subjects;

Junior NCO's No. 1 at Tidworth

Map Reading and Geography

Junior NCO's Drill Cadre at Tidworth

Junior NCO's Rifle and Lewis Gun Cadre , Tidworth

Army 1st Class Certificate in Mathematics.

By the end of 1936, I played rugby football and cricket for the regimental teams and was in the Novice boxing team. As a result, I did not go abroad but stayed in England to compete against other regiments and the forces that had teams such as the Air Force, Fleet Air Arm and the Tank Corps.

At the beginning of 1937, I was promoted to Corporal and transferred to the Motor section of the regiment. As the infantry units were now being motorised, I was sent to the Tank School at Bovington, Dorset for three months where I trained in repairs and maintenance with a variety of vehicles, tanks, armoured cars, motorcycles and Bren gun carriers. I was awarded certificates of distinction in both practical and theory, returned to my regiment and in December was sent to the Morris Motor Factory in Birmingham. There I was to oversee and learn about the types of vehicle which were being made for the services.

I worked in civilian clothes and was billeted in Small Heath with a lady named Mrs. Dimbleby. Her husband had been shell shocked in the first world war and was still in a mental establishment near Birmingham.

Upon my return to my unit, I found that great changes had taken place, Lewis guns had been changed to Bren guns, 'One' Company had been made into Support Machine Gun Company with Vickers water-cooled machine guns and Bren guns were beginning to arrive.

It was also the time of the year when the army prepared and trained for presenting items to the Tidworth or Aldershot tattoos which were great spectaculars. My regiment was training for two items, the first a massive Indian club demonstration where the clubs were lit at the end with lights of different colours from batteries inside each club. This was done in complete darkness, except for the clubs, and about three hundred men were involved. It was a fine sight.

The second contribution was to be a performance of the story of the British army climbing the Heights of Abraham to take Quebec in Canada, which was at that time held by the French. A massive structure had been built to scale and the Royal Welch were portrayed attacking, dressed in their red jackets. The Royal Berkshire regiment was dressed in blue to represent the French.

The two regiments were great rivals and there were some very funny things happening in that attack which weren't rehearsed. There were make believe men being shot, tripped up and rolled down the hill, the tall black hats of the French soldiers flying through the air. It did look good from the stands and by all accounts the show looked quite authentic.

One day before the actual show started, we were being marched by a Sergeant Lander to a rehearsal at the showground. Near to the stadium there was a small group of officers talking together, Sergeant Lander shouted "March to Attention", meaning 'eyes front' and no talking. Someone ahead of me was still talking and the sergeant, thinking it was me, pushed my shoulder and shouted "Shut Up". Immediately, I said to the man next to me "Did you see that?", to which I received the reply "Yes Corporal" and we carried on marching.

For days afterwards, the sergeants seemed to be avoiding me and Lander was looking positively ill. What I learned later was that it was a Courts Martial offence to strike a soldier and that Lander thought I was going to charge him with striking me. About a week later, the sergeant major of my company came to me and asked me if I was going to charge Lander. I said "What for?", I've no reason to charge him. He replied "Thank you Corporal, I will let him know."

About a month after this episode, I was made up to Lance Sergeant and on entering the Sergeants' Mess,

Lander was the first to shake my hand and to say thank you. It appeared that if he had been charged and found guilty, he would have been discharged from the army, his wife and children would have to leave married quarters and he would have lost his pension. I then understand why he hadn't looked well.

In 1937, I became a member of the regimental boxing team and boxed against the Royal Scots Fusiliers and 11th Hussars as a light welterweight, winning both fights on points.

In 1938, the team won the Aldershot Command Inter-Unit competition and I was presented with a cup and medal. I still have the medal. The cup decorated our living room for many years but unfortunately it eventually succumbed to the enthusiastic play of my three children as they used it in their childhood games.

In 1938, I was promoted to sergeant and put in charge of the Bren gun carrier platoon. This was composed of ten carriers with three crew to each carrier, one corporal or lance corporal as senior member, one driver and a gunner. The senior member acted as No. 2 as well as being responsible for the vehicle.

In six months, the crew had been trained in attack and defence, in support of infantry, camouflage and movement at night. Taps or pressure on the shoulder or steel helmet were silent signals to the drivers. The V-eight engines of the carriers were so quiet that it was possible to manoeuvre quite close to an enemy position before being heard.

Just before Christmas 1938, my CO sent for me and said that he had received a letter from an amateur boxing promoter in London with a request that we enter a few of the team in an amateur competition in Walthamstow Baths, London. The CO suggested that I take three others for the event and then go straight home on leave for Christmas.

Of the men I took with me, one was a middleweight, one welterweight, myself at light welterweight and a bantamweight. What the CO had not told us but we found out when we arrived, was that it was a knockout competition. So if we won our first bout, it meant we fought again and possibly again to the end.

Our bantamweight was first in the ring. He lost on points. I followed and had six bells knocked out of me, cut lip and rapidly closing left eye. Welterweight lost on points. Middleweight, bout stopped in the second round as he was virtually out on his feet.

We had thought we were good but we were not in the same class as these people. We had time to spare so we stayed to watch the rest of the bouts.

The chap who had beaten me was boxing again, he was doing very well but was then knocked out in the second round. He didn't regain consciousness and was carried out on a stretcher to the dressing room and the doctor was called to him. The boxing had finished when the fellow came round, most of the chaps who had fought that night sat around and watched.

The doctor gave the man a thorough inspection and then said to him "When did you last eat, son?". The recovering man said that it had not been for two days as he had wanted to make the weight for his bout and wanted to win the silver cutlery tray which had been the prize. He planned to sell it and give his wife and children a good Christmas.

He received a good telling off from the doctor, but enough money from the rest of us to ensure that the family did indeed have a reasonably good Christmas.

When I arrived home the following day, the first remark from my mother when she opened the door was "Whatever have you done to your face?". I replied that I had been boxing in London but it didn't hurt .

In 1933, when I had joined the army, I had signed on for seven years with the colours which meant that I was an active soldier living in military quarters and could be sent on active service any where I may be needed for a period of seven years. I would be in the army reserve for an additional five years after that and could be called on at any time during those five years to serve my country again in a time of national emergency. I was now in my last year and undecided whether I should take on for another term. It was possible at that time to take the last six months away from the army, learning a trade. It was that which I decided to do and applied to the Spitfire factory in Southampton to train as a Spitfire aircraft mechanic.

I was granted leave of absence with pay and allowances for food and I found myself digs in Southampton with a lady who was a flower arranger on the big sea-going ships. At this time there were rumours of war and Mr. Chamberlain, the then Prime Minister, was visiting Hitler and others in Germany over concern with rapidly worsening relationships on account of Germany flouting treaties and its ill-treatment of Jews in that country and Poland. Chamberlain returned to England announcing "No war in our time".

This left me in the Spitfire factory trying to make an old piece of metal into a perfect square about half an inch thick, with sides of around three inches. My party piece was another gem – I was to make a nut and bolt out of scrap alloy which should fit together perfectly. Sadly, the first attempt was not quite square and when the nut and bolt were finished, they were not really partners, you could drive a horse and cart between – no, fly a spitfire through the gaps.

Fortunately for the Spitfire fraternity, on the Friday before war broke out (Sunday 3rd September 1939), I received a telegram from the War Office ordering me to return to my regiment which I did immediately. With the other men who had been similarly recalled, I sat on my bunk bed waiting for Mr Chamberlain to make the announcement that we were now at war with Germany. The announcement duly came.

CHAPTER FOUR

Military life does continue!!

The next day I was back in uniform. The CO sent for me and told me that I had been a fool to leave the regiment as I had been doe for promotion to sergeant major. In addition to that, I had been replaced as sergeant in charge of the Carrier Platoon and the man I had trained was taking over.

Within a week, we were on our way to Southampton and then on to Cherbourg. On arrival there, I was put in charge of about thirty reservists who had been called back and I was moved from our staging camp to another, marching the men about twenty miles a day until we reached St. Marguarit de Pornichet on the southern Brittany coast close to St. Nazair. We put up tents in a sandy area wooded with fir trees – reminiscent now also of quite contrasting family holidays with growing teenage children!!

Within a further week, we had established an organised camp with guards, cooks and the necessary communications back to the regiment and higher authority.

A young officer fresh from Sandhurst was sent to run the camp with me but I rarely saw him. I had organised the men on paper according to their training and their skills. It was the time of the 'Phoney War' and the regiment was spread along the Belgian border near Tournai, digging trenches, machine gun and mortar pits and laying barbed wire.

When men were sick or hospitalised, I would send replacements up to the front which extended south to join up with the Maginot line, held by the French army.

The Maginot Line was a series of concrete fortifications which were constructed between wars one and two to deter a German offensive into France. It accommodated large and small artillery and places for defending soldiers and gun crews with sufficient food and water for them to start a long siege. It ran from Switzerland to the Luxemburg and Belgian borders.

Around the end of November, Sergeant Arthur Carr who had taken over from me as carrier sergeant, went sick with boils on his neck and I was then ordered to report to the regiment. I didn't get even a chance to see the carriers, however, as immediately, I was engaged with my men in digging trenches etc.

The winter of 1939 was bitterly cold and we were billeted in a barn with only one army blanket and an overcoat each for warmth. The farmer who owned the barn gave us a bucket of hot water each morning in which thirty or so men had to wash and shave and so for the sake of hygiene, we issued each man a half mess tin of the water.

I agreed that pairs of men could share their blankets to afford them extra warmth. I did notice that those that shared put their overcoat on first before tucking down beneath the blankets.

At the end of November 1939, my brother Roy was called up for National Service training and was still in England. My sister Beryl was in her final year at Pontllanfraith Grammar School and had applied for teacher training college at Crewe.

I was given 10 days leave and a week before Christmas set off for Calais to get on a boat for Dover. All went well and I eventually boarded the South Wales from Paddington to Newport. About 5.00pm, the train halted in Reading and we were informed that the line had been bombed just outside Didcote and that there would be delays.

Many of the passengers went to the buffet car for refreshments and after a short while, someone started to play the piano. Before long, there was a party going on which lasted until well after the buffet should have closed. We then returned to our carriage which was freezing cold and tried to settle for the remainder of the night. Before we could get much sleep, however, the train eventually left Reading and I arrived in Newport just in time to catch the Sithowy Valley connection to Pontllanfraith.

This train was nicknamed 'The Rodney' , the name given to unruly or misbehaved boys, as it was the first train of the day that carried milk and fresh fish plus 'the drunks' who had failed to catch the last train home from Newport the night before. It went north up the Sirhowy Valley dropping supplies along the way.

That Christmas, I met Margaret Evans, Beryl's friend from school who eventually became my wife.

After Christmas, I returned to my regiment and continued with my men to dig mortar pits and trenches and to use barbed wire to protect them. One freezing cold day I took delivery of a number of corrugated iron sheets which were to be used to reinforce the bunkers. At the end of a bitterly cold day's work, I marched the men back to their billets and dismissed them. The next morning, I was sent for by the commanding officer and charged with neglect of duty. It appeared that at the end of the day, he had flown over the area to inspect the work which had been done and where I had been working, a new sheet of corrugated iron had been left outside the trench and which could be plainly seen from the air. As charged, I was found guilty and "severely reprimanded". That would be recorded in my records.

About a week afterwards, the young officer who had been made 'Carrier Officer' came to see me to ask how the men were and particularly to ask about the carriers which were parked up in the village square. I told him that I had not seen them for two months and that in all probability, the batteries would be flat and that, because of the heavy frosts, if the war really started tomorrow, we would not be able to move them from the square.

He must have told the CO because I was sent for and asked "Do you accept the responsibility for the statement you have made about not being able to use the carriers?". I responded "Yes Sir", and he replied by saying "You have twenty four hours to get them off the village square and report to me. My men worked the twenty four hours on two hour shifts and four hours sleep. We took the tracks off the carriers to get at the brake drums with blow torches and sledge hammers to free the brake shoes from the drums so that the vehicles could be steered.

One by one the batteries were checked, put into a warm environment for an hour or so, boost charged and then refitted on the carriers which were started and driven for about five miles until they were ready for inspection. My CO came to see me and congratulated us on the work we had done. I was then told that I was now Brigade Carrier Sergeant and that I was to visit the other two regiments in the brigade to get their vehicles back on the road. I was also made responsible for training the crews to replace casualties. I was transferred to brigade headquarters and within about a week had started my new job.

Shortly after these events, my diligent CO made another inspection flight over the battalion's defensive positions and his plane was shot down by a German fighter aircraft and he was killed.

Towards Easter 1940, the defensive positions had been completed and retraining started with vigorous run and march routine, route marches with full kit and patrols from the Maginot line into Belgium. Troops were ferried to Douai in batches where they had showers in special buildings erected by the Royal Engineers, they got their hair cut and all uniforms were put through heat treatment machines to kill any vermin that may have been picked up. For the first time, at weekends, all ranks except those who were on duty and confined to camp, could apply for a pass to visit nearby towns.

By the end of March, visits to Lille and Douai were made regularly when organised groups went for their showers and so on. Our individual units made up football teams to play local French sides and a great deal of fraternity was going on with the local girls and our soldiers. War seemed a long way off.

At Easter 1940, I was given another period of leave and spent most of it back in South Wales with Margaret Evans. She and her sister Trissie (Beatrice) were on holiday from Swansea Teacher Training College and so was Beryl from Crewe. There was little really to do, the cinema, the local dances and visits to the local pub seemed to be the highlights of 'the valleys'. There were blackouts from lighting up time in the evening to dawn the next day. Petrol was rationed which seriously restricted travel and bus and train services were curtailed.

When I returned to my unit after leave, I took with me a framed photograph of Margaret and a promise that whenever possible we would write to each other. The photo went with me in my pack when I was on the move, by my bedside when in billets. It has in all seen service in France, India and Burma and become soaking wet on numerous occasions. When the war finished, I had it refurbished and framed, and to this day, it is still with me.

On the 10th May 1940, the war started in earnest, the Germans crosses the borders of Holland and Belgium and pincer movements were made around the Maginot line which caught the French armies virtually facing the wrong way. The British Expeditionary Force (BEF) were on a front from Dunkirk in the north to Sedan which was the northern end of the Maginot line. The BEF were ordered to advance, including the R. W. Fusiliers which was heading for Brussels led by the carriers. At this time, I was at brigade headquarters with my reinforcement drivers and gun crews waiting to move forward. Only snippets of news were coming back from the front.

Well before Brussels, the leading carriers ran into anti-tank fire and three went up in flames losing all the crews. Then, between us and the forward troops, German paratroops were dropped which isolated us from the regiment. Reports were now coming back of heavy casualties and soldiers of the French army were coming back without their arms.

The brigade major who kept me up to date with news from the front, sent for me and said "things are not going very well – we have sustained heavy casualties and the French have capitulated. You must pick up a party of replacement soldiers plus your own men and make your way to Dunkirk". The replacement soldiers were young men who had done only about eight weeks training and then been sent out as reinforcements. I gathered them all together and gave each one a bandolier of .303 ammunition and two hand grenades. We then set off for Dunkirk which was about 60 miles away to the south west.

Twice on the road, which was crammed with refugees all fleeing from the German advance, we were bombed and strafed. Each day, we marched about 15 miles. About half way to Dunkirk, we ran into heavy artillery fire and, expecting an attack to follow, I placed the men in defensive positions near a wood telling them to keep their heads down to prevent them being spotted from the air.

At regular intervals, I visited each section to make sure they were OK. It was a very hot day and when I arrived at one section, the corporal in charge said he had one lad who was very upset, he was in tears. I asked what the trouble was and was and the lad told me that with the extremely hot weather, he thought the grenades and the ammunition would blow up. I reassured him that this couldn't happen but it did leave me wondering what how they would react should they be attacked.

I had another sergeant with me who really was not a fighting man. I've really no idea why he joined up with me, he was known as 'Skipper Jones', was short, plump, red faced and had a moustache with spikes. He was a liability in so much as wherever we stayed for the night, a barn or whatever, he took his dental plate out and carefully secreted it away somewhere. The following morning, before we could leave and continue our march, we would all have to search for his teeth and could not set out until they were found.

Eventually, we arrived at Dunkirk. It was being shelled, strafed and bombed continuously. We joined the queue on the beach and after about four days wait, my group had reached the water's edge. After what seemed like a very long wait in this spot, I was picked up in a small boat with some of my men and put onto a larger vessel in the harbour. When on the large boat, which had been a sheep transporter before coming here, I and the others were ordered to go below, and then still further below.

Then a voice from up above shouted down to us "Is there anyone who can use twin Lewis guns against aircraft down there?" and I duly responded because I I could. I meant that I could travel wherever it was we were to be going above deck and in the open air instead of being trapped below decks. We soon left for England and fortunately I was not called upon to fire at any aircraft. We arrived at an English port complete with crew and passengers all safe.

When the boat docked, the first passengers to leave were the wounded who were on stretchers followed by the walking wounded. Everything was done in an orderly and disciplined fashion. There were quite a large number of French airmen, sailors and soldiers who had joined the queues on the beaches at Dunkirk. These were led off by military police until their identities had been checked as they could have had German spies amongst them.

We walked from the dockside to a long train waiting nearby and when full it pulled away into a station platform. Military police came along through the train and ordered everyone to stay in the carriage they were in. Within minutes, trollies pulled up alongside with two or three Salvation Army ladies to each one. We were served with sandwiches and tea, the first real food we had eaten for days, and, best of all, there were sheets of writing paper, envelopes and pencils handed into the carriage. We were told to write a short note to our parents or next of kin to say that we were back in England. The letters and pencils were then collected up by the ladies, and the letters posted for us. There was great rejoicing in my household when the letter arrived as my parents had previously received a telegram from the military saying that I was "Missing, believed killed".

After these formalities, the train pulled away from what we later learned to be Dover station. After travelling all

43

night and part of the following day, we stopped at a large station and by listening to the accent of the people on the platform, I realised we were somewhere near Newcastle. I was immediately ordered, along with my men, to leave this train with other groups of soldiers and to board a smaller one in the next platform.

We pulled away and travelled for a good hour or so before stopping and then we were ordered to leave the train. We were told that arrangements were being made to find temporary billets for us all. Before long, there were un-uniformed men and women arriving on the platform and the local police. I was asked to fall the men into ranks and I went along the lines with the people as the police asked them in turn "how many can you take?". As they answered one, two or three and so on, I would select the appropriate number of men from the line and off they all went until the platform had been cleared.

The only one left unallocated was me and a policemen said "you had better come with me sergeant" and he took me home with him. I will never forget that bath, hot water and scented soap, soft towels and to crown it all, egg, bacon and fried bread with pots of tea. The next day, I felt embarrassed as I realised that I had been given their week's ration of bacon and eggs.

The events of the previous few weeks seemed to have been a nightmare. Looking back to the incident of the corrugated sheets and subsequent events, I believe that had these not happened, I would have been leading the carriers along the road to Brussels and that I would have been one of the first victims, along with my crew, of the German anti-tank gunners.

The people of the town of Consett, near to Newcastle, were very kind and generous. Quite a few of my men had worked in the mines back in South Wales and Consett was a mining and steel town. We therefore had a lot of ground in common. The locals even fitted my men out with rugby kit so that they could play against their sides. While all this was going on, I and my men were transferred to a church hall which became a collection point for all the Royal Welsh men who had arrived in the area.

A major from the regiment came to the hall and suggested that I make out a programme of training for the men to

a) save them from getting bored and

b) prepare them for possible invasion by Germany.

Every man had saved his rifle and bayonet and a few had their bandoliers of ammunition but no grenades. We marched and ran alternately 100 yards of each for three miles every morning and did rifle drill in the afternoons.

I cut a hazel rod from the hedgerow about seven feet long, put a padded knob on one end and a wire ring on the other. This was used for bayonet training. The men formed a circle around me just out of reach of the stick, then I presented either the ring or the knob end to them, moving quickly around so that they could bayonet the ring and use the rifle butt to hit the knob as I turned. This was going quite well until a local lady ran onto the green where we were performing and started hitting me with her umbrella. I warded the lady off with my hazel rod and she kept repeating "stop shouting at those boys" and

45

tried to hit me. By then we were attracting quite a crowd and I had to show her that I was not trying to hit the boys but was teaching them to stab the ring at the end of the stick or thump the ball at the other end to prepare them for a possible German invasion. We ended up being loudly applauded by the onlookers and the lady went away looking very red faced.

A few weeks after this, I was ordered to take the men to Middlesborough to another, but larger church hall. This was one of several points where the Royal Welsh from all over the country were told to report. We became a regiment again with new officers, non-commissioned officers and men, many of whom had only recently completed their initial training and had not experienced any action.

When the numbers had grown significantly, the whole regiment was transferred to a housing estate in Bridlington, North Yorkshire. Here, once again, we were used to build bunkers, mortar pits and trenches and the Royal Engineers mined all the beaches except the parts where the local fishermen manoeuvred their boats in and out of the water. Britain was preparing to repel an invasion but the major problem was the lack of equipment, much of which had been lost in France.

To help out, whilst the soldiers were preparing our defences, a citizens army was formed. It was initially named "The Local Defence Volunteer Army" but was later renamed "The Home Guard". It was made up of young men considered to too junior to serve or who were unfit, and also those who were too old. At that time, there were a few who were armed but most weren't, so the remainder would carry wooden replica rifles or farm

46

implements which could be used for drill training. For many years, they were the butt of music hall humour (later, Dad's army, for example).

After Dunkirk, a number of German aircraft were retained on airfields in northern France in order to harry the seaports in the south of England and the shipping in the English channel. This was planned to disrupt as much as possible the delivery of much needed supplies to Britain. This prompted Air Chief Marshall Sir Hugh Dowding, commander-in-chief of fighter command, to reorganise his forces in a pretty short period of time. He was short of fighter planes and having lost 300 pilots in France, he was forced to bring men earlier from the training schools. He also borrowed pilots from the Fleet Air Arm, the Canadian Air Force and also men who had escaped from Poland and Czechoslovakia who could fly.

By the beginning of August 1940, the regiment had completed its work on the beach defences which started south of Bridlington and continued south a distance of about 10 miles to the village of Skipsea and covered all the suitable landing area in the region.

A day before we left there for a rest period, a general came along to inspect our work. Having done so, we were congratulated on the speed and quality of our efforts. We saluted each other and he moved on. Not many minutes later, there was a loud explosion from the beach. Rushing to where the noise had come from, we found that the general had stepped on a land mine and been blown up. All we found was his red cap.

The following day, we arrived at a village of Beeford which was a sleepy little place with two pubs and a sweet shop, about ten miles from the coast. I was fortunate enough to be billeted with another sergeant in a garden shed belonging to a family in the village and most of the troops were in bell tented areas in orchards and woods on the nearby farms.

We were enjoying ourselves one Saturday evening in the pub when someone rushed in and shouted "The church bells are ringing". There was a stunned silence for a few moments then, in seconds, the place was empty. Ringing church bells was the signal that we were being raided and there were orders to the effect that if and when we heard this, everyone was to report back to the unit immediately and certain duties were performed in preparation. One of mine was to fuse boxes of grenades. I went to the barn where they were stored with the ammunition and five of my men carried the boxes out into the open air. Then with the light form torches, we put the fuses into what seemed an endless number of grenades.

All duties were eventually completed and we bunked down. I was kept awake be the realisation, however, that we had all been drinking that evening and what would have happened if we had mishandled one of the explosives.

The next morning, we were informed that the bells had sounded out a false alarm and that we were to defuse everything, including the grenades and re-store as before. This time it was all done very, very carefully!!

The following day, a German reconnaissance plane flew low over the area about nine o'clock in the morning. It didn't fire a shot or drop a bomb and to everyone's surprise, went away as quietly as it had come. The short respite from the bombing which came after Dunkirk was soon over and German aircraft resumed their "Blitzcrieg" tactics as they had done in Spain and Poland. They came over in droves accompanied by fighters and where we were in Yorkshire, Flamborough Head jutted out into the sea and was an easy landmark for aircraft.

The German long range fighter, the Messerschmit, was not able to match the British Spitfire or Hurricane in combat, however, and each day during the Battle Of Britain, more and more German fighters and bombers were being shot down.

Early in September, about fifteen German bombers with fighter escorts came in at around fifteen thousand feet and, out of the blue, came the British fighters only visible by the tracery of their vapour trails high up in the sky. The Germans were losing so many aircraft that they were directed to concentrate their efforts on just bombing London and the surrounding areas. By the beginning of September, however, our RADAR was so effective that as the bombers met together over the French coast in preparation for their bombing raid on London, the fighters were alerted to them and they had already taken off and gained sufficient height to deal with them.

Hitler and his generals had made plans to invade England. But on 17th September 1940, because of the heavy losses of German aircraft, the plans named "Operation Sea Lion" were postponed. Daily, the newspapers printed the numbers of enemy aircraft shot down and it began to read like a cricket score – "185 for 6". "Operation Sea Lion", the invasion of Britain, was then postponed 'indefinitely'. On 18th December 1940

Hitler revealed his plans for the attack of Russia, codenamed "Barbarossa".

The Battle of Britain had been won. Of the total 3080 pilots involved in the battle, more than one in five had been killed. Of them, Churchill made his now well known statement "Never was so much owed by so many to so few".

In November 1940, the regiment was transferred to Malton, a small town close to the Yorkshire moors. Our training became more intense, marches in full kit became longer and longer until forced marches of fifty miles were being done in all weathers.

The young men who had been drafted in after Dunkirk were well trained but still had not seen action. Just before Christmas passes were given for home leave and they continued to be issued until everyone had spent their two weeks at home. I was fortunate in that my ten days covered the Christmas period which I spent with my family. Beryl was home from college, Margaret and her sister Trissy too. Because of the uncertainty of the future, Margaret and I made no plans but agreed to write as often as we could.

The Hunt Ball - Malton

Whilst in Malton, a colleague, Sergeant David Roberts and I visited most of the pubs in Malton and had decided that the best of them all was The Brewers Arms. As there was no sergeants mess, whenever we came off duty, we would wend our way to The Brewers. The

50

locals were generous people and we were frequently invited to tea with the families of friends we met there.

B Company, unlike the rest of the regiment, were not billeted in the town but about three miles outside, along the road to Thirsk. The house, a large rambling building, needed a lot of attention and was surrounded by hills occupied by a large number of sheep.

The owner of Middleton Manor gave us permission to use one of the hillside fields to run in the newly fitted low-noise tracks of the carriers.

When we were taking a break at the B Company kitchen, we were introduced to the huntsman who looked after the Middleton hounds and who was there with his son, Matthew. We arranged to meet up with them in the Brewers a couple of days later.

On the appointed day, we arrived at the Brewers as planned and met huntsman George who was accompanied by Matthew, his daughter Anne and her friend Gillian. In the general conversation, we learnt that Gillian had bought four tickets for the East Riding Hunt Ball which was being held at the Bridlington Spa Pavilion the following Saturday. Matthew was unable to go as he was taking the station wagon to York that day. Gillian's friend a lad named Dennis in the RAF had been posted to Cornwall, so he was out too. Sadly, it meant no escorts for the girls and no transport either!!

It was time for my 'brilliant' idea – I could leave a Bren Carrier at B Company HQ, borrow two steel helmets and two greatcoats for the girls and then David and I could act as escorts. Yes, they could go to the ball. On the night, we donned our steel helmets and greatcoats and drove to Bridlington without seeing any other transport. We parked up the Carrier with steel helmets and coats inside at the rear of the pavilion. David and I had borrowed shoes from Matthew and his father as we had only had ammunition boots, and with these, we danced the night away.

At the end of the evening, we dressed up again and set out on the journey back. About three miles from home, we came across a convoy of army lorries parked without lights on the roadside. I panicked. I stopped the vehicle and told the passengers to put their helmets on straight, chinstraps under chins, and coat collars turned up. I then continued at a steady pace.

We came to a group of officers carrying maps and miniature torches and with them, a tall military policeman, all standing in the middle of the road. I slowed down as I drew near to them and the policeman indicated with his light that I was to get a move on. I did as I was bade, getting out of the way as quickly as the vehicle would take us but I did notice that right near him were two staff cars with flags on their bonnets.

We dropped the girls off and returned to our billets. I saw David the next morning whose immediate words were "Do you know who was holding that roadside conference last night?" which, of course, I didn't. "It was General Montgomery." He concluded with great glee.

Early in the spring, I was pleased to get a visit from my brother Roy. He was stationed in Suffolk and had been given a few days leave. We were able to spend a weekend together and then, shortly after his return, he was posted to Egypt. I didn't see him again until 1944.

The German bombers were less frequent now but did continue their bombing raids on a smaller scale. They came in smaller numbers but were often driven off before they had even dropped their payload of bombs. At sea however, 1939 to 1942 saw the loss of thousands of tons of British shipping along with much needed supplies from America. Most of the damage was being done by German surface warships and submarines that hunted together in packs. Britain had an arrangement the U.S. under what was called the "Lease-Lend Agreement" between the two countries whereby America would supply Britain with food and other necessities to be paid for by Britain at the cessation of the hostilities. America was not at war with the Axis countries until Japan bombed Pearl Harbour on 7th December 1941. After this it then became a conflict with Germany, Italy and Japan fighting against Great Britain and America, we were no longer alone.

Then our fortunes changed, first to go was the German battleship, the Graf Spee, sunk by British warships in the river Plate, South America. Then came the sinking of the two German battleships, the Gneisenau and Sharnhorst, the pride of the German navy. The Bismarck was soon to follow. Of its 2400 crew, British ships picked up 119 survivors.

Unfortunately the flagship of the British navy, The Hood, was lost in the battle with the Bismarck, the captain and full crew being lost with the ship. These victories marked the end of German warship raids against convoys in the

Atlantic. Their submarines, on the other hand, still posed
a very great danger.

In late spring 1941, my regiment moved from Malton to
Cheltenham racecourse buildings with the officers
billeted in the town. As our temporary homes were
within the confines of the racecourse, we were free to
wander anywhere, even into the 'Silver Ring' on race
days assuming we were not engaged in training
exercises. On Gold Cup day, I went down to the ring just
to have a look around and watched the bookies setting
up their stands and taking bets. There was one tall
young man working at one of the stands with the bookie
who stood with a bag over one shoulder and a bunch of
tickets in his hand. The bowler hated lad said to me "Are
you going to have a bet, Sergeant?" to which I replied
that I knew that horses ate grass and that was about all I
knew. He said "When the racing starts, I am going to
make a bet with another bookie, you follow me and listen
to the number of the horse I'm going to bet on, then you
go to a different bookie and bet whatever you can afford.

I followed his instructions all the afternoon and when I
saw the amount of money he was putting on the horses,
I increased my own stake. I won handsomely, coming
away from the afternoon over a hundred pounds in profit.
A few days after my win, I went home on 48 hours leave,
Beryl was there and I was able to buy her a few dresses
and bits to take back with her to college.

On my return to camp, training continued as usual, long
route marches over the Cotswolds. We had to put up
bivouacs made from groundsheets and we were issued
with a piece of meat, small portions of vegetables, Oxo
cubes and had to cook our own meals in mess tins. We

ate quite a lot of half cooked food as the wind and rain upset our cooking plans.

We then went through a period that not only confused the enemy, but which confused ourselves too. We were told to assemble at predefined times at the quartermaster's stores where, to our great surprise, we were fitted with white blouses and matching white ski trousers, white linen caps and again, white gaiters. All these we had to label up with name, rank and number and then pack into a plastic bag and return to stores. This prompted a great deal of speculation about the location of our next move and as the German army had already occupied Norway it seemed that that was where we would be going. We were cautioned not to tell our families about any of this, or to mention it to strangers we met outside in shops, pubs and so on.

A month later, exactly the same thing happened except this time, the clothing was khaki drill and pith helmets and as the war in North Africa was hotting up we assumed now that this would be our destination rather than Norway.

On Sunday 22nd June 1941, the German army invaded Russia, the operation being known as 'Operation Barbarossa' and the attacks by ground forces were preceded by heavy bombardment by the German air force. As a result of this new move, and the knowledge that the Germans were committing vast numbers of men and arms to the Russian front, we were quite relieved to learn that there would be no threat of Britain being invaded for quite some time, if ever.

Christmas 1941 came and went and the type of training changed, we took part in Brigade and Divisional exercises which involved large numbers of troops. We practiced equipment movement, bridge building by the Royal Engineers, river crossings by foot and barge. Platoons of thirty men were taken to Gloucester and loaded into planes with equipment and ammunition. They were flown to another airport, unloaded and joined in further exercises on the ground.

In February 1942, we were taking part in an exercise which started in Suffolk and after one day supporting an attack that appeared successful on paper, I with my Carriers were ordered to move. We were, with Carriers and along with another Brigade, to form a defensive line about five miles west of Hull. We arrived there about 5.00 o'clock in the morning, taking up positions as ordered.

Suddenly, without any warning, as though it was part of the plan, the port was bombed, first with incendiaries which were then followed up with high explosives. The bombing lasted about twenty minutes and from where we were, the whole city seemed to be on fire.

I received an order by radio to move eastward with my men and equipment towards Hull and to rendezvous with others about a mile from the town. Unfortunately, after we had moved only a mile or so, a very dense fog descended upon us, I lost radio contact with my unit and decided to stop until first light.

The following morning, visibility was not good but we were near enough to Hull to smell the burning. When it was possible to see for a distance of about eighty yards,

I saw, to my horror, that we had run over a bowling green and made a dreadful mess of it. I felt I had committed a crime and was unable to find anyone to whom I could apologise.

Saint David's Day With The Royal Welch Fusiliers

The 1st March in the Royal Welch Fusiliers is a holiday for those who are not on duty in recognition of the patron saint of Wales, Saint David. It is a day when the officers of the regiment serve breakfast to the other ranks (those below the rank of sergeant) and a day when the youngest recruit in the regiment eats a leek to the rolling of a kettle drum.

After breakfast, when the dining room has been cleared, the youngest recruit is paraded before an audience of his peers, the CO, Officers, Warrant Officers, Sergeants, the Regimental Goat in all its finery, the Goat Major, and last but not least, a drummer with drum and in full regalia.

The recruit stands on a bench seat with one foot on the table, the drummer starts to play rolls on his drum. The Commanding Officer hands the recruit a chalice containing a number of short, trimmed baby leeks about five inches in length. The recruit takes hold of a leek, raises it from the chalice and announces for all to hear "A Dewi Sant" and in English "And Saint David" which is repeated by the audience. The recruit is then offered a chalice of beer, or should the ceremony take place in the Officers Mess, a chalice of champagne.

The leek is consumed and washed down with ale or champagne and the whole audience cheers to end the ritual.

In 1942/43 when all the 1st Battalion were preparing to fight the Japanese who were rapidly advancing through S.E. Asia, members of the Regiment wrote articles of interest which would be published in a paper named 'The Informer', distributed amongst the Companies.

The following poem was written by Lieutenant David Graves, (son of Robert Graves, author). David was posted "Missing, believed killed" March 18th 1945.

Ode To The Difficulties Of Celebrating St. David's Day In A Foreign Clime In A Proper And Fitting Manner

What is there in this land accursed

With which to honour March the First?

The goats round here are far from royal,

Pot-bellied, small and unhygienic

Not wishing to appear disloyal,

Our uniforms are far from scenic.

We aren't allowed to sport the Flash,

To wear red coats and cut a dash

We cannot now pomade our hair

And wigs are definitely rare.

The pioneers are drably dressed

It really makes me quite depressed

The long white gauntlets might be worn

To ward off wounds from barb and thorn.

But clean, white aprons would be stained

In jungle streams and forest saps

And camouflage would not be gained

When searching huts for booby traps.

So I suppose that battle dressed

Our pioneers get on the best.

Occasion seldom here occurs

For wearing Toby Purcell's spurs

The only things to ride are bikes

Which do not get on well with
spikes.

Our leeks will just be lengths of
marrow

Cut down to shape and long and
narrow

With good whole sauce as some
disguise

These may achieve complete
surprise.

A new boy now is far to seek

There's precious few to eat the
leek

To put one foot upon the table

And say as well as they are able

"A dewy Sant" – Gulp – "And Saint
David".

Proposing healths in neat palm
toddy

Appears to me a trifle shoddy

"A Dewy Sant" in fine dark port

Is rather what I feel we ought

And then the toast "The Ladies" seems

Harsh probing of nostalgic dreams

And "Guests" will be replied to by

Unasked intruders from the sky

Dropping their cards just after dinner

When talk is wearing slowly thinner.

But we will do the best we can

And vent our feelings on Japan

And may we be, next March the First

Far distant from this land accursed.

**** The End ****

CHAPTER FIVE

Movement at last?

At the beginning of March 1942, there was a feeling in the air that we were due to move again. It became reality when my CO sent for me and ordered that I was to prepare all carriers for action and to make sure that all equipment was packed securely for journey by sea. I was to take the men in Carriers to Gloucester railway station, load them onto the flats with the remainder of the Brigade Carriers, wheeled vehicles and ambulances.

We were to stay with the train and wherever the destination port, we were to remain there until the ship was fully loaded. Two days later, we arrived in Glasgow and were directed to a park with Nissan huts for accommodation and a cook house to feed us. The remainder of the park was full of vehicles.

The name of the ship was the 'Oranji'. It was very carefully loaded so that if we were going into action, the vehicles which would be needed early on, i.e. tanks, were nearer to the top. Ambulances went right down below.

Each day for about a week, I marched the men from the park and down to the dock in the morning and then back to the park at the end of the day. About the third day, we had just left the dock through the main gates when a large dray, pulled by two horses and loaded with crates, came towards us. It was being driven by a big woman wearing a leather apron.

Alongside the road, there were the usual dockside railway lines and the woman guided the horses and dray to one side to allow us more room. Unfortunately, however, the nearside wheels of the dray caught in the railway lines and the dray tilted over. This caused a crate to slide off which hit the road and startled the horses.

It was the first time in my life that I had heard a woman use bad language and it came as a bit of a shock. Even the men went quiet.

The week or so that we had in the docks was very interesting. In the next dock to the Oranji was the US aircraft carrier 'The Eagle'. It was massive and made our boat look like a toy. It was part of the convoy in which we were to leave England and one of the biggest convoys ever, excluding D-day.

At the beginning of April 1942 the convoy left Glasgow, I was on the command ship and all my men on the Oranji. The command ship had originally been the "Empress Of Japan" but when the actual Empress of Canada had been damaged, the Empress of Japan became the new Empress Of Canada. We headed out from Glasgow not knowing what our final destination would be.

When we were out of sight of land and well into the Atlantic, as far as the eye could see all around were more ships. Leading were the destroyers, and darting about like little sheepdogs behind were a number of other smaller naval craft. The flanks were occupied by

63

motor torpedo boats for a day or two and then they turned and went back to England.

We still didn't know where we were heading but the training continued nonetheless. About ten days out from the UK, all officers on board ship were called to a meeting in one of the dining rooms where the news was broken to them that we were going to take Madagascar from the Vichy French both because they controlled the islands, and because they were working hand in glove with the Germans. They were giving shelter to German and Italian ships which were intent on sinking British shipping on route for trading purposes to India and the Far East.

Every day the training program went on with all troopships in the convoy. At any given time, it was possible to know where people were - top deck, march and run in full kit wearing plimsoles instead of heavy boots, physical training and games – bottom deck, study films of defensive positions on Madagascar, wireless training, signalling and so on.

When we got near to Gibraltar, a third of the convoy left the main group and went into the Mediterranean, escorted by warships and the Ark Royal aircraft carrier while we carried on south along the west African coast.. Not long after entering the Med. On 23rd April 1942 the carrier was torpedoed and beached. Margaret's brother Douglas was on board at that time and jumped from it onto a destroyer before it sank into shallow water.

Some three weeks after our initial departure, the convoy pulled into the harbour at Freetown in West Africa. After looking at nothing but sea for all that time it was a welcome change to see the coconut palms, the tin roofs of the buildings and the red soil of the land. The local people came out to meet us in their small boats loaded up with bananas and oranges but we were all forbidden to buy anything from them because their standard of hygiene was regarded as suspect.

The native boys in the boats nearest the ships would dive into the water after a coin was thrown down near to them. It was possible to see the shiny coin jiggle to and fro in the clear water as the boy swum after it. The coins rarely escaped them.

The convoy refuelled in Freetown and both days that we spent there, for about ten minutes there was torrential rain. As we were washing and bathing in salt water while aboard and using salt water soap to enable us to do this, the rain was a welcome treat to have the heavy shower of fresh, soft rain for us to wash all over. There were about fifty Alexandra nurses aboard with us during this time but come the rain, they would all miraculously disappear.

Prior to 1800 whenever servicemen went abroad there was little or no help for the families left behind. If men were wounded or killed there was no pension for wife, little financial support or medical help for the wounded until 1885 when a Colonel Sir James Gildea, with the backing of Queen Alexandra arranged for the training of nurses and the donation of funds to help returning soldiers and sailors. Since that time "Alexandra Nurses" in the armed forces have melded to become a well-trained and disciplined organisation. They could, until the end of the 1939 – 1945 war be recognised by their white headdresses, red capes and military bearing.

At Freetown, we received more aerial photographs of Madagascar showing where their defences were located and more briefings took place on which were the best ways of dealing with them.

Another two weeks and we had completed the journey along the west coast of Africa down to Capetown. From the docks there we could see the tops of the tall buildings on the foreshore and behind them the backdrop of Table Mountain, a very impressive sight. The day after docking we paraded on the dockside in full marching order and with the band playing, marched off to the west. On the outskirts of town, the band stopped playing but we carried on for another twenty two miles ending up at a police training depot on the coast. We found accommodation for the officers, a tented camp site for the NCOs and men and plenty of washing and showering facilities.

After showers and first inspection, all men were given permission to swim in the sea before having their meal. The sea looked supremely inviting and as we didn't carry bathing suits, we all galloped down the beach 'starkers' towards the water's edge. This didn't really matter as the place was off limits to ladies. But as many of the men hit the water, there were howls from all along the beach, including from me. I have never been in such cold water in all my life. We did manage to overcome the shock of the moment with a truly excellent meal followed by an offering of boxes of all the wonderful fruit that South Africa can grow laid out before us to select from. Compared to the dried then stewed fruit which we had enjoyed for breakfast week after week aboard ship, this really was a memorable treat.

That evening, most of the men spent a couple of hours in the bars while the drinks were varied and comparatively cheap. This was a jolly evening but no-one was looking forward to the march back to the Empress Of Canada early the following morning.

By dawn the next day all the men had washed and breakfasted and by seven o'clock were paraded ready for the return march. Many were suffering from extreme hangovers and others were not talking to their fellows. Our company set off with the company Commander in the lead and me at the rear. This was at times not a good place to be on account of the effect that all that alcohol mixed with fresh fruit juice was having on the digestive system of the troops!!

About a mile along the road I got 'rescued' by a despatch rider who drew up alongside me and said "Get on behind please Sergeant, the C.O. wants to speak to you." I climbed onto the back of his motorbike as requested and as I was doing so began to think what on earth I had done the previous evening to incur the wrath of the Colonel. I didn't have to wait long. I was taken up front of the column and dropped off so that I could talk with the C.O.

I saluted him and said good morning. He returned the salute and then said "I want you to go back to the ship and make out passes for 24 hours leave for all the men of your company. They must be signed by the duty officer of the day before being issued."

With great relief I replied "Yes, Sir", saluted him and got back onto the motorcycle which took me directly back to the ship in dock at Capetown. There, I felt as relieved as if I had been released from prison. My guilty conscience, I suppose!!

Back on board, the passes were completed and I had them signed well before the troops returned. I was able to enjoy a good forty winks before they actually arrived.

On arrival, they stowed equipment and arms, had a shower and were paraded for foot inspection. By the time this was completed, a meal was ready for them and passes made out ready for issue. I looked out while this was going on and saw that there were cars pulled up on the dockside with many men and women standing around chatting together.

As the men walked down the gang plank, a lady or gentleman talked to them and on arrival at the quay, one, two or three men would join that person as they walked over to their car, climbed in and drove away. I realised as I watched that the people of Capetown were offering the men hospitality for their 24 hour period of leave ashore.

I descended the gangplank with two other sergeants, Thomas, Signals and Davies, Mortars. A lady with a girl aged about 16 was waiting with another man and woman and as stepped down onto the concrete she announced "this is my daughter Angela and my brother-in law and his wife, Richard and Grace. We share a home and would be pleased if you would come and spend your leave with us". Their home was a magnificent suburban colonial-style building with a swimming pool in the palm tree lined back garden. We hadn't been there very long before we were given swimming shorts and towels and asked to join the family out on the 'stoop'. There we sat outside shaded from the burning tropical sun sipping fresh chilled orange juice and wine between swims.

That evening after a really slap-up meal of locally caught fish with sautéed sweet potatoes and a selection of fresh and colourful local vegetables, we were taken out by car on a trip around the town. We saw the silhouetted outline of Table Mountain flanked by its sentries Devil's Peak and the Lion's Head, a truly glorious sight that remains in my mind's eye even today. The twinkling lights along the tree-lined back of the 'Sleeping Lion' or Signal Hill as it is better known, absolutely breathtaking.

We drove up to Tambour's Kloof the gateway between the city and the Twelve Apostles and the lower cape that lies behind the peaks. From there we looked down one way to the city lights below and the sea beyond with ships at anchor in the harbour. Behind us the other way lay Camps Bay and Moulle Point with its flashing lighthouse right on the sea front, and then beyond, sea again past Robben Island as far as the imagination could go.

The trip out was concluded with a stop at a fairground where we spent about an hour sampling the rides before returning home for drinks prior to going to bed.

As we had been driven around, we learned from the general conversation that our hostess, Mary's husband Geoffrey had been take prisoner by the Germans whilst fighting in the desert with the British Army.

I will never forget how generous these people and the others that we met and heard about from the men, were, and I understand that every convoy of British soldiers that docked there received the same welcome and treatment.

The twenty four hour pass unfortunately expired and we reported back to the ship, harboured in the dock as we had left it just the previous day. Of the eight hundred men and NCO's who had been given leave, three of them failed to return and were posted as A.W.L. to be relentlessly sought by military police. One of these was in my own Company, an unsavoury character who frequently had to be scrubbed by the others as he continually failed to keep himself clean. More of him later!

We left Capetown as a convoy about an hour before sunset. As we built up speed on our departure from the harbour, the sun went down as a red ball and disappeared below the skyline. We were then in complete darkness and although we could see nothing at all, the sounds of other ships reminded us that we were indeed part of a convoy and not alone.

Suddenly and unannounced, there was a huge explosion that came from some distance out beyond the stern of our vessel. It reverberated across the water and the echoes from the sides of the other ships could also be heard. After this, it all went absolutely quiet again and we were left wondering what on earth had happened.

The following morning, we were told that the 'Oranji' carrying my men and the Brigade's carriers and other transport had either been torpedoed or had hit a mine. Either way, it was gone, lost. We were also informed that that we would no longer be going to take Madagascar but had changed course for Bombay, India.

70

Looking out at the other members of the group, it was obvious that we really were significantly fewer in number. Next to us, a safe but reassuring distance away, there was a destroyer. It would stay for a while and then assume a similar defensive position alongside one of our sister ships.

While this had all been going on, our training sessions continued as far as they could but our other routine duties had been changed, officers and NCO's being involved in new things. My own newly allocated responsibility was on the edge of the catwalk. Armed with a very large and efficient pair of binoculars, I was on submarine watch from dawn to dusk, two hours on, four off.

As we progressed further from the African coastline and into deep and totally unprotected ocean waters, it became very rough and the swells so high that the destroyer, sailing along about two miles away from us, would disappear as it dropped down into large troughs. But like magic, it would reappear every now and then and through my binocular lenses, I could just make out that the visible crew were all attached to their ship's railings.

In approximately ten days we were nearing India, the sea changed from a clear blue with white caps to a sullen grey. There was also a distinctive smell in the air that I had been told about by others who had visited India before. Into view came the 'Gateway of India', their equivalent to the Arc de Triomphe in Paris but much smaller and standing proud out on the sea front.

We docked but were not allowed ashore. We could see the 'real' India but were not allowed to touch! The heat was searing, the humidity exhausting. We could smell that foul water odour with maybe a hint, possibly imagined, of oriental spices mixed in. We could see the frenzied activity down below us on land. But we would have to wait.

Nearby there was a ship being coaled. Doing this there were women, with their saris tucked into their waistbands, walking from a coal dump up the gangplank, a basket of coal balanced confidently on their head. They dumped their load of coal, turned and walked off the ship by a second gangplank – and this continuous business went on ceaselessly for hours.

On the shore we could see a gang of labourers moving a long piece of railway line. There were eight men each side of the iron rail working in pairs with the man the other side. Each man held one end of a rope which went under the rail and then into the grip of his partner. The foreman, who walked along to one side, chanted a couple of short and rhythmic lines that ended on an emphatic and final beat. This acted as a signal to the men to lift and swing the rail, to the same rhythm, a forward distance of about two feet, in time for the foreman to then continue his song.

I learned later just how cheap labour was out there and those in the railway work gang would have been paid an absolute pittance. Unfortunately under the caste system which was endemic in India at that time, people of low caste were poorly educated and only able to obtain work in the more menial of tasks. The low caste was a source of cheap labour and their wages very low. Ghandi referred to them as "The Children of God".

Later in the day we disembarked and moved into a tented camp near the dockside – 'Colabor' camp – and in order to leave the camp for the city of Bombay, it was necessary to go through the dock gates on which there was an armed guard.

Before the men were given passes to go out into Bombay, talks were given to them by Englishmen who were members of the Indian police. They covered a number of topics including thieves and pickpockets, Indian customs and traditions, brothels and venereal diseases, areas where it was unsafe to venture particularly alone or after dark.

Amongst an average Company of soldiers there are always the thinkers, the jokers, those that can turn a serious situation into a funny one, those that can turn a funny situation into a serious one and so on. Within days of being in Colabor camp, duty rosters were drawn up for guard duties and other routine tasks that had to be done or supervised. It came up my turn on guard duty.

The number of men in a guard depends on the number of points to be guarded. In the case of the dock gate, one sentry stood right by the gate with bayonet fixed and he was accompanied by a civilian Indian policeman to open the main gate for vehicles, secured it behind them and then ordered the drivers to report into the guardroom.

Passes for the men were always made out for a return deadline of 11.59pm, so like Cinderella, they had to be back in camp by midnight at the latest. Outside the dock gate there was a Tonga rank where two-wheeled, 2- or 4-seater horse drawn tonga vehicles with driver could be hired to take people into the city.

After 10 o'clock pm it was usual that men returned to the dockside in varying states of drunkenness, reported to the guardroom and then went to bed. Around 11.30pm on one particular night when I was not on duty, there were voices raised outside the gate and a policeman came in, happened to see me and asked me to intervene. When I got to the gate I heard someone shout "Hip, Hip" and a number of voices joined in with a chorus of "Hurray". This happened three times and then three men came to the gate calling "Goodnight" back away from the gate.

The sentry stopped the men and asked them what all the fuss was about and they replied that they were just thanking the tonga driver. The Indian policeman followed their explanation in fairly good English with a more accurate interpretation, namely that they had not had enough money to pay the driver so were giving him three cheers as a thank you.

The men were taken into the guardroom where their names were recorded together with the amount they owed – three rupees (about four shillings then) In today's rates there are about 80 rupees to the pound so the amount owed was not really significant but it was a principle of honour. I paid the driver his fare and took it back from their pay the following Friday.

For some time then, Ghandi had been calling for the British to leave India and return government to the Indian people. He was a pacifist and believed in passive resistance. A number of his followers were not pacifist, however, and were actively attacking locations in Bombay which were part of the British Raj and authority. Our duties extended to guarding places like the cotton mills which were British owned but employing a large Indian workforce. Railway stations were attacked and trains sabotaged.

Not only were they attacking British interests, they were also quarrelling with other local sections of the population who were not Hindus. Each morning, a large 30cwt (1 cwt or hundredweight = 8 stone = 112lbs) truck, covered with a tarpaulin would be escorted around the streets by our troops to pick up the bodies of those who had been murdered during the night.

Piano wires were stretched across streets leading to government establishments where dispatch riders were in common use and they were positioned at a height to cause maximum damage across the throat.

There was a police rest house sited at the centre of a city square where four streets converged and this was used by off duty police for resting purposes. We were called out from a mill that we were guarding because petrol-soaked rags had been thrown into the rest house. By the time we arrived, it was too late, the fire had got a hold on the building which, without proper fire fighting equipment, was doomed.

The English policeman who was with us beckoned "Come on, I know where to find the people who've done this" and we followed him dutifully. We patrolled both sides of the street seeing post boxes on fire one after the other until it stopped near a barber shop. The policeman fired two shots at the door lock and then kicked the door open. As he did so, men came out of the doorway like rabbits with a determined ferret at their heels.

As one individual stepped onto the street from the building, the policeman shouted "That's him", shot missing intentionally and announced firmly that he would get him eventually.

Not long after this event, Ghandi was put under house arrest in a bungalow near Poona (see later!). We often saw him taking the air with his ladies in its grounds.

Wherever there were troops in the Far East, particularly in India, there were "Char Wallahs". Whether the men were in billets or tents, the char wallahs, with permission from the CO, would sit in a shady spot somewhere central and dispense the 'char' (tea) from a large metal container. Beside the large tea urn was usually a large wooden tray with a cloth draped over the 'wads' (cakes) that were also for sale. The price charged for char and a wad was always fair. At mid-morning and mid afternoon breaks, he can be found selling his char and wads.

By Wednesday of each week there were many soldiers who had been to town too often, were stressed for cash and resorted to seeking credit from the char wallah who kept a little book known as the 'Katab'. The soldier would get recorded in the Katab the number of chars and wads that he had consumed on credit and then he would sign against the record. On Fridays, pay days, he was expected to settle this debt with the char wallah.

At the end of the first week in Colabor camp, the char wallah came to the Company office on the Saturday morning to complain that there were men who had not paid him. There was a parade at 2.00pm and I asked the wallah to be at the parade with his Katab. I had seen the book and knew what to expect. I stood the men at ease and said I would like the following men to take one pace forward. I then called from the Katab the name of each man who had not paid up – Mickey Mouse, Clarke Gable, Henry Hall and so on. This initiated great laughter amongst the gathered troops but those owing the wallah started coming forward to settle up with him. Every single person ended paying up and even the char wallah finished with a laugh when it was all explained to him. That never happened again while we were there.

MOHANDAS GHANDI, MAHATMA ('GREAT SOUL') 1869 – 1948

Gandhi was the father of independent India and one of the most outstanding personalities of the 20th century. The young Gandhi was betrothed at the age of seven years and married in a non-sexual relationship at fourteen. He was educated in India then studied law in England, eventually becoming a lawyer and politician in South Africa.

At the age of 45 he returned to India and concerned himself with the plight of the untouchables, peasants and mill workers who he felt were discriminated against. He organised strikes and work to rule walkouts, and devised a non-violent civil disobedience campaign. Initially, he didn't oppose British rule in India but when the British passed an act perpetrating the curtailment of Civil Liberties, he escalated his activities against the government.

He was arrested and imprisoned several times by the British on such charges as sedition in 1922 and when he led a month long protest against the British salt tax. His imprisonments had the opposite effect of what the British had in mind. Gandhi became a larger figure as a result of being imprisoned and gained more influence in the country.

Gandhi also gained notoriety and influence when he organised hunger strikes to protest against violence in India. During the 1920s and 30s, religious violence between Indians, Muslims and Sikhs began taking place. Gandhi was a firm believer in religious tolerance and began hunger strikes to try to have his fellow Indians listen to him and end the violence. Furthermore, violent mobs attacked military outposts (most of the soldiers were in fact Indian, not British) killing several soldiers.

379 people were killed in one incident by machine gun fire from the governing authorities.

He staged hunger strikes to protest against the violence, arguing that it was not beneficial. In 1931, he had enough recognition for the United Kingdom to invite him to London for talks that would possibly give India its independence. The talks broke down, however, and Gandhi returned to India where he continued his work and where he would spend the rest of his life.

In addition to fighting the British rule in India, Gandhi began to represent the 'untouchables' of Hinduism, the lowest caste in Hinduism. It was a sin to even touch them. Gandhi began to protest against their treatment and started referring to them as the 'children of God' in attempts to elevate their status in society.

Gandhi and his wife were put under house arrest in Poona because of their activities, the ruling authorities having concluded that his activities here out of control. His wife, Kastur, died there in 1944. Gandhi was released in May 1944 as his health had started to decline, He spent 2,338 days in prison during his lifetime. (Approximately six and a half years)

On August 15th 1947, India became partitioned into three areas to quell the communal strife between Hindus, Muslims and Sikhs.

On January 30th 1948, Gandhi was shot, the apostle of non-violence died by violence – but not before blessing his assassin. His body was cremated on the banks of the sacred Jumna river at New Delhi and his ashes scattered over the gently flowing water.

80

CHAPTER SIX

Getting settled In India

After Gandhi was placed under house arrest in August 1942, things soon got back to normal and the regiment moved east from the camp to Ahmed Nagar, a semi-hill station set in a dry and arid area to the north east of Poona (now Pune). During the day in the dry season, it becomes very hot indeed and because of the midday and afternoon extreme heat, we did our training in the mornings and rested in the afternoons.

We started to acclimatise ourselves to the sun by stripping to the waist and working out in the direct sunlight, first week five minutes per day, second week ten minutes. Anyone who got sunburnt was in serious trouble as it was officially classed as a self-inflicted wound.

When the acclimatisation stage had progressed a number of weeks, pith helmets were discarded and replaced with bush hats. Spine Pads were withdrawn from service and equipment worn on parade was reduced to a minimum. From this starting point, the process went the other way, gradually the weight of equipment was increased again until the men were training in the heat of the day and in full marching order.

On 15th February 1942, Singapore had surrendered to the Japanese who continued their advance to the west and north. Those folk, soldiers, civilians, men, women and children who escaped from Singapore started their retreat to the north and eventually to India.

The nature of our training, meanwhile, remained much the same as training at home in England. At that time we were not thinking of jungle training but talk was beginning on stopping the Japanese before they could get to India. Our training continued, we had open air film shows in the evenings and concert parties and acts from England came to entertain the troops. Vera Lynn was the most popular of those I saw.

The main concern of most men was that of how their families back in England were coping with the German bombing and the rationing of supplies. The war in the east still seemed a very long way away.

On September 1st 1942, my commanding officer, Lt. Colonel Humphrey Williams, sent for me and asked whether I might consider taking a commission. I had refused once before as it meant going to officer training school and after passing out I could be posted to anywhere but my own regiment. This time he assumed that I wished to stay with the Royal Welsh and went ahead and made an appointment for me with the Divisional Commander.

The Commander was a very kindly person, he asked about my background, education, parentage and so forth and after about 20 minutes of interview he announced to me "You may return to your C.O. and tell him that with effect from tomorrow, 2nd September 1942, you will no longer be Sergeant Bennett but 2nd Lieutenant John Bennett.

On return from my promotion, I moved from the Sergeants Mess to the Officers Mess and was greeted warmly, particularly by my friend of many years, Captain

Douglas Lyman, second in command of his Company. We were both fusiliers training at the R.W.F. depot in Wrexham in 1932/33. We had both come a long way since then.

Today as I write these words, it is in the year 2003. So more than 60 years have passed since Doug Lyman welcomed me so warmly into that Officers Mess. Today, he is still my great friend, living now alone in Shropshire in the same bungalow that he and his wife Hilda shared for many years until her untimely death in 1969. His health has failed in recent years and he is more or less confined to within the house these days. But that doesn't stop us enjoying our regular weekly phone calls and me taking his bets each week over the phone and placing them at my local bookie's shop. We've been doing this for years now, the profit held by me and funding all the stake money. I go and stay with Doug maybe twice a year which gives us both a chance to sit and chat over old times and at the same time enjoy a tipple or two. We don't know how long this will continue now as time marches on but for sure, we will savour every minute of what is left.

Because of my length of service and experience, I was promoted to Lieutenant just a few weeks later on and made Carrier Officer. One of my men, a good soldier and always very well turned out, agreed to be my batman. We were together in France and Dunkirk and I knew that come what may, I could trust him.

I hadn't been in the Officers Mess very long when Roberts, my newly appointed batman, came in and informed me "There is a native at the door asking for work and his wife does 'Dhobi' work". I went outside to see the man and asked him what he did. He called himself David and said he would carry water for the sahib, clean shoes and equipment etc. for 2 rupees a week (about 15p). His wife, he explained, did laundry.

I had always liked to have clean, white, nicely ironed handkerchiefs so I told Roberts to give him any soiled ones of mine and for him to David to return them as I liked them. Before leaving, David took off the red fez that he was wearing and removed from it a smutty roll of pieces of paper which he thought were testimonials from previous customers. The first one, however, read "Watch him, he's a thieving sod. Signed, Donald Duck" and the others that followed were all in the same vein. Roberts liked David and so we took him on probation.

Some days later, I was sat at my table writing a letter home, David was cleaning boots out on the verandah while Roberts was preparing my equipment ready for the following day. I heard Roberts say to David "You lazy bugger, I told you to get the sahib's water ready, he has to be in the Mess by 7.00 o'clock". David's answer came in a very pompous and deliberate way, "I not lazy bugger, I bloody Christian". On another occasion, I heard him tell Roberts "Oh, yes, Queen Victoria very nice man".

In November 1942, we were granted leave. Camps were set up at Mahabaleshwar which nestles in the curvaceous mountain ranges of the western ghats of Maharashtra, and also at Bombay. NCOs and other ranks could spend their ten days holidaying there, food provided by the army.

I, with two other officers, Lieutenant Jim Cunning and Lieutenant Ellis Jones, travelled to Kashmir which lay due north from where we were beyond the Indian border. We went into Bombay, boarded a train there which travelled for three days to Rawalpindi on the northern peak of India and adjacent to Islamabad.

We then went by taxi from Rawalpindi, still travelling north, across the border and into Kashmir. From Rawalpindi, the road climbed through the Murree Hills until we were up into the foothills of the Himalayas. The roads were cut into the side of the mountains, were quite narrow and had a drop of thousands of feet to the valley below where the Jumna river flowed through. The taxi driver drove like a bat out of hell, not knowing what was around the corners, bullock cart or bus or animals, he went at the same speed for two hundred miles. It was seriously frightening.

For the period of our leave while not travelling, we lived up in the hills on a houseboat, one of may similar ones moored on a lake and connected to land by a rickety boardwalk. It was sheer heaven. There were lilies all around the lake and fish of all shapes, colours and sizes could be seen in the crystal clear waters around the boat. The location was held in a backdrop of distant mountains which seemed to get higher and higher the further away they were.

About a hundred yards out towards the centre of the lake there was a large, two storey houseboat which operated as a restaurant and a bar. It could be reached by boat or by swimming. Small craft circulated the lake calling on the occupied houseboats and offering to sell diamonds, silver and gold trinkets and jewellery at prices much cheaper than in the cities.

Although it was hot at that time of year, away in the distance we could see that the higher mountains were all snow-capped. It was an idyllic place to spend that leave period swimming, drinking cocktails, dining and relaxing in the shade from the sun. When it was time to return, it really was a wrench to get up and go.

Leave over, we drove back down that dreadful roadway with the same mad driver and after three days we arrived back in Ahmed Nagar tired but pleased to have made the effort to witness such a wonderful land. In the cold weather from October to March, the climate is perfect for military exercises and games and we did plenty of both. There was a lot of practice on the firing ranges where troops did simulated attacks beneath overhead machine gun fire. There were also attacks under creeping barrages of twenty five pounder shells which exploded two hundred yards in front of troops making for an objective. Special groups were also trained in the use of flame-throwers and one of my carriers was converted into a mobile flame thrower.

On the weekends, there were intermittent games of soccer and rugby football. In one such game when we were playing in the final against another regiment stationed in Bombay, I was playing scrum half and went to gather a loose ball with my right hand at the same time as someone else decided to kick it. Instead of the ball, or as well as perhaps, my hand which was under the ball and against someone's heel, my hand took the full brunt. This resulted in a broken wrist, two broken fingers and one other dislocated.

Fortunately, the hospital was local and I was put into plaster up past my elbow. This did curtail my activities but I could still take part in work that involved the carriers.

We learned quite soon after these events that it was planned by those in command that we were to be used to stop the Japanese invasion of India. The training therefore intensified.

Some weeks later with my arm still in plaster, I was asked to attend a meeting which included a Brigadier and his Adjutant, a Colonel from the Ordnance Corps and other senior representatives from the regiments in our (6th) Brigade. We were briefed that…

the main thrust of the Japanese army was coming north along the west coast of Burma.

inland from the sea about twenty miles was a long mountain backbone and when the rains came, the rivers flooded. The paddy fields on the lower slopes of the hills were always flooded - our forces would need transport and other armoured vehicles in these adverse conditions to carry supplies and men these means of transport would need to float.

Experiments were being carried out on various forms of wheeled transport and each Regiment in the Brigade was ordered to provide a Bren Gun Carrier for the ordnance division to adapt. They planned to seal every nook and cranny on the vehicles so that they would float across flooded clearings and rivers. The vehicle that we had furnished was eventually returned duly modified and a date was set for our visit to a reservoir named Cappa Wadi tank about twenty miles away.

The carrier had to be equipped with its normal operating load and crew. My CO took me to the tank in his staff car and on the way asked me whether I thought the modified Carrier would float. I had to reply that I thought not and gave for a reason that, even though it was sealed, there was not enough flotation area and that the weight of its bullet-proof steel composition would sink it.

The Carrier was driven to the water's edge by my driver then the Brigadier told the two crew members to get out and he and his aid-de-camp replaced them in the vehicle. The army photographer stood ready with his camera. The Brigadier tapped the driver on his helmet and said "Drive forward slowly". The carrier moved slowly forward as the water gradually crept up along its side. As it advanced further into the water, it continued to stay firmly on the ground and as the water got deeper less and less of the vehicle remained visible. The driver, Brigadier and his aid stuck resolutely to their assignment until the Carrier and they had completely submerged leaving just two red caps afloat on the wadi.

The driver was lifted out and taken to the bank and the other two swam ashore on their own having realised rather late in the day that the experiment was an obvious failure. At the time, no-one dared to be caught smirking at what had happened, everyone struggled to maintain a straight face. But later in the evening in the Officers Mess, the event was recalled and retold in the spirit of amusement it really had deserved.

CHAPTER SEVEN

The Longest Retreat

Just before Christmas 1942, we received our marching orders. The Japanese were heading north taking towns and villages along the way. It was obvious they were now heading for India.

Some significant chronology...

1941

7th Dec.   Japanese attack Pearl Harbour

8th Dec.   Japanese land in Malaya. Allies declare war on Japan

25th Dec.   Hong Kong falls

1942

15th Jan.   Japanese invade Burma (now Myanmar) from Siam (Thailand)

15th Feb.   Singapore surrenders to Japanese

7th March   Rangoon falls to Japanese

1st May   Japanese capture Mandalay

On 30th April 1942, the British withdrew beyond the Irrawaddy river and then the Chindwin river. The long contingent of soldiers, civilian refugees, men, women and children of all ages, many sick and starving, who had travelled a thousand miles fleeing from their oppressors, arrived in Imphal.

As they crossed into Assam and reasonable safety, the monsoon broke and gave both Japanese and British forces an opportunity to replan their future tactics. At about this time, the First Battalion R.W.F. with 6th Brigade of the 2nd Division, made preparations for their advance on into Burma. My orders were to take the battalion carriers to Bombay, load up a train with them plus ambulances and other vehicles together with many boxes of varied ammunition. I was in charge of the train, the crews and everything on board.

The journey took about a month to progress the whole way across India from Bombay to Calcutta. We stopped at all the major towns and cities and were often put into sidings to allow express trains to get past.

Each day I radioed forward to arrange for food to be loaded on board and to arrange facilities to stop and get the men bathed and toiletted. After every stop, there was a headcount to ensure that none of the hundred men I had started with had disappeared. All the vehicles were on 'flats' and when the train stopped, it was easy to walk from the rear of the train right up to the leading engine unit. This was also done quite often when it was time for the men to brew up tea or other drinks as the engine supplied all the hot water. During this time, I also learned to drive the train and how to apply the brakes.

Whilst sitting in sidings one day, a tall Indian man wearing a smart turban walked along beside the train. With him he had a small boy and on his shoulder sat a small monkey. He stopped near me and said "Salaam sahib" and I replied "Salaam". He asked me if he could do tricks with the boy and the monkey and I agreed. As he started, the men saw what was happening and gathered to watch. It was one of the finest exhibitions of agility and timing I have ever witnessed.

The men showed their appreciation by giving small coins to both the man and the boy and then returned to their places on the train. The man then looked up and said to me "I can tell your fortune for cha anna's (which was a small coin worth $1/16^{th}$ of a rupee). He asked me if I had a 'mem sahib' and when I replied that, yes, I did, he looked at my palm for a while and wrote something on a piece of paper saying to me "That is the initial of your mem sahib, please keep it in your pocket". He told me that I was going into danger (obvious really!!), and that I would be hurt but that I would return. There were other less significant things too said to me.

When he had finished, he said to me "What is mem sahib's initial?" and I replied M for Margaret. He then told me to take the paper and look at what was written on it. I took the folded paper and opened it up. The initial he had written was indeed M for Margaret.

Our next stop was the holy pilgrimage city of Benares, now called Varanasi. When nearing the city, we stopped on the girder bridge which was astride the river Ganges, holy to the Hindus. In the evening sunshine, the tops of the golden temples shone with an unsurpassed brilliance, and as the sun went down, the gold turned to red and slowly disappeared. As the lights came on along the embankment, they and the silhouetted building line made a most beautiful sight.

The previous day I had radioed ahead and arranged for a day in the siding so that we could take on rations and the men could clean up and get some exercise. In the morning, some of the men asked permission to go swimming. They went but were back very quickly having learnt that bodies were burnt on the 'Burning Ghats' on the embankment, but that those of the poor were often were thrown in unburnt as the could not afford to pay.

When I left Bombay, I had understood that the rest of the regiment were to have been entrained two days later that us and that they would journey on to Calcutta and then Chittagong, the port for northern Burma. While at Benares, I went to the military headquarters to try and find out where they were but was merely told they were "still in transit". I did learn, however, that the Japanese had been halted at a village called Donbaik, that they were dug into bunkers and the first attempts to dislodge them had failed.

In the meantime, I was having fun and games with the Indian railway system. The strategic communications in India were designed for me to cover the north west frontier but the threat now was coming from the south east. The major obstacles to our communications with Assam and Burma were the Ganges river and the even larger Brahmaputra river and its tributaries.

The movement of freight and vehicles from Calcutta necessitated unloading the train at the Ganges and ferrying the vehicles and ammunition across. On arrival at the other side, the railway changed from broad to narrow gauge, back to broad guage again up to the Brahmaputra. Here again, we had to unload the train and ferry everything across once more.

It was very hard on the men but they were aware of the necessity and the urgency of the situation and worked hard at loading and unloading.

The last hundred miles was done by road and on arrival at Chittagong, we met up with the Regiment which was spread out in woods on the outskirts of the town. 6th Brigade was composed of four regiments each of approximately 800 officers and men:

2nd Battalion, the Durham Light Infantry

1st Battalion, the Royal Scots

1st Battalion, the Royal Welch Fusiliers

1st Battalion, the Royal Berkshires

All four regiments had trained in special tasks in connection with amphibious operations such as the invasion of Madagascar, but none had trained for jungle warfare. None of the generals in India commanding troops fighting in Burma had any experience of jungle warfare methods, strategy or equipment.

All that officers carried in action was a revolver with ten spare rounds of ammunition. Each man carried a Lee Enfield rifle which was cumbersome and too large for jungle use, particularly with a fixed bayonet.

When in action, officers soon acquired Tommy or Sten guns and demands were made on rear echelons as these smaller arms were accurate up to two hundred yards.

We were also in need of shorter fused grenades. Ours were fused for ten seconds which meant that if thrown a short distance, they could be returned before exploding. This did sometimes happen.

We remained hidden in the close confines of the fir trees for a week, awaiting the arrival of a cargo ship loaded with essential equipment. Each night it became very dark as the sun set and the only lights in the woods were those of the cooks still working after feeding everyone or at the Battalion and Company HQ where meetings were being held.

Gradually, the lights extinguished one by one as the activities drew to a close and as this happened, the world went very still and quiet. On one of these nights, in the darkness a mouth organ suddenly began to play accompanied by someone else who could whistle as well as an oboe or a flute. The men began humming along to the tunes, but soon the whole camp was in full song to the familiar tunes of Wales – "Land Of My Fathers", "David Of The White Rock", "Cwm Rhonda" (Guide me o' thou great redeemer) and many other old favourites. At times I could feel the hair on the back of my neck rising and even today, when I think of those evenings in the woods, it still does.

After unloading the ships cargo in Chittagong port, it was loaded onto our vehicles and we got on the move. My carrier did escort duties each day and guard duties at night. This ensured that the marching troops got a good night's rest ready for the following day. Reveille was at 5.00 o'clock each morning and the men, having breakfasted and cleaned up, were on the road by 7.00 am in the cool of the day. Every day, they covered ten to fifteen miles bringing them closer to Cox's Bazaar!!

CHAPTER EIGHT

The Arakan Theatre Of Operations

The Arakan area stretches from the south of Chittagong to the small Burmese port of Akyab, a distance of approximately 200 miles. A few miles south of where we were was the peninsula end known as 'Foul Point'.

To the west was the Bay of Bengal and the coastline features varied from partial mangrove with swamp and mud banks to partially sandy, surf-ridden beaches. The peninsula was about thirty miles wide south of Chittagong and just a few hundred yards wide down at Foul Point. Down the length of the peninsula was the Mayu Ridge, a mountainous spine, jungle covered and rising to a height of about 1500 feet, very high for such coastal geography.

The hills were deeply cut by numerous water courses which during the rainy season became raging torrents running down into the Ganges and out to sea. Beyond the Mayu range was the Mayu river and jungle covered hill tracts inhabited by head hunters.

When we arrived at Cox's Bazaar, we were told that the Japanese were in Maungdaw which we had planned as our next stop about seventy miles south.

We stayed at Cox's Bazaar for two days where everyone bathed, shaved and washed underclothes etc. and spent any remaining time cleaning and oiling weapons and machinery. Our stay over, we then set out south for Maugdaw. After travelling about three miles, we were all halted and sitting in the shade of the trees when the whistles blew to warn of aircraft approaching and we all went for cover. Looking up through the tree tops, we saw two large flights of Japanese aircraft, about twenty five in each flight. They were in arrowhead formation, one behind the other and heading straight for Cox's Bazaar.

Suddenly, the leading plane fired a long burst of machine gun fire and then the whole flight let loose their load of bombs. We could hear the 'crrrrump' far away as the bombs exploded and then we saw a large cloud of black smoke billowing up into the sky. We assumed that a petrol dump had been hit and realised just how fortunate we had been as the Japanese seemed to be targeting the very outskirts of Cox's Bazaar where we had just spent our jungle rest days.

We knew that there were both Indians and Burmese who were in the pay of the Japanese, aiding and abetting them by feeding them information such as day to day troop movements.

When we were within ten miles of Maugdaw, reports started to come in that the Burma Rifles with supporting Indian 5th Division troops had cleared the Japs out of the small port and forced them to retire south onto the peninsular. They were digging themselves in near the village of Donbaik.

The Japanese had withdrawn back to a large water inlet named FDL Chaung. The chaung was fed by water from a stream which rose in the Mayu Ridge and it was also filled by the sea at every high tide. It was a natural obstacle which had been utilised and improved upon by

97

the Japanese having dug a system of mutually supporting weapon pits and bunkers along nearby.

The bunkers were hollowed out of the ground, roofed with large tree trunks and covered with 5 feet of soil. When they were attacked, their machine guns did not fire at specific targets but across the front of the bunkers. Any attacker would have to pass through lethal fire. They also shelled and mortared the tops of their own bunkers to thwart attacks from above.

The British positions were reminiscent of first world war trenches with sand-bagged parapets in a jungle setting. They were separated by twenty yards of chaung from the extremely well camouflaged Japanese positions.

When we eventually arrived in Maungdaw, the Royal Engineers were already rebuilding bridges that had been destroyed by the Japanese and they were making use of 'coolie' labour to break up rocks for road repairs. The roads were mainly dirt and fine for bullock carts but totally unsuitable for military traffic particularly during the monsoon period when they would be flooded, slippery and unstable.

We stayed in Maungdaw over the 1942 Christmas period. On Christmas day we had chicken bought locally and potatoes and vegetables that had been dropped by parachute. This was followed by Christmas cake, made from Army biscuits and currants, and which tasted like cardboard and was mostly thrown to the birds. The whole affair was rounded of with a very welcome and enjoyable tot of rum.

Christmas afternoon, my crews played football with an elephant's turd but this halted abruptly when a dog-fight started up overhead. We couldn't see the aircraft, just the vapour trails as they twisted and turned in the air as they manoeuvred for advantage. There were intermittent bursts of machine gun fire as this continued and then suddenly, out of the blue (literally!) appeared a parachute with a pilot swinging underneath. We couldn't see whether it was British or Japanese as he headed towards the jungle canopy and landed about a mile to the south east of our position.

After the Christmas period in Maungdaw, we started moving south to what was commonly called "Bandit Country". Each Company (of four in total) had three carriers as escort and another three carriers were used as escorts for Battalion HQ and ambulances as we progressed. Every village, hut, bamboo clump and area of jungle was searched or patrolled. Quite often we were fired on by snipers or Japanese patrols as we went along and these had to be found and dealt with before the Companies could again move forward.

The enemy also had one or two artillery pieces which they must have dismantled and carried in parts, by either men or mules, to the top of the Mayu Ridge. When they fired down on us, our artillery would work out their probable location, helped by any useful information we could radio through to them, and then reply with a barrage of shells. The British artillery were twenty five pounders (shell weight) and were located about five miles to our rear, escorted by infantry units.

The Japanese also had a spotter plane that sounded like a sewing machine when it came overhead. We were ordered not to fire on it as it would give our position away – there were several occasions when I could have blasted it to bits but it was not to be done. It was obvious the Japs must have known where we were anyway because when we stopped for the night, usually on a hillock or other high ground, their infantry would come close and shout "Give in Tommies, your wives are at home having fun with the Americans".

During the hours of darkness, they fired tracer bullets onto our positions to give the impression that they were attacking. Another ploy was that in a lull in the fighting, a voice would cry "Help, help, Tommy, please Tommy" as though it was one of ours who'd been hit. One day, the movement forward was halted...

...And I received a wireless message to report to the C.O. at Battalion H.Q. When I arrived there I was told that B Company, who were holding the flank in the lower jungle on the Mayu ridge were losing a man every five or six minutes, being killed by a sniper. I was told to take six men, find him and get rid of him. Being a Welsh regiment, we had an advantage over the British and Indian Regiments, as our C.O. spoke Welsh and the wireless operators spoke both English and Welsh. I asked him to let B Company know that I was going to operate to the north of their area, and gave him the reference points where I would be working, and said there would be wireless silence until I was able to open up again.

I had selected an area to start the search where the trees were highest, as I would have put a sniper where he would have a good field of fire, and there was concealment. I planned that the men who wore canvas topped rubber soled boots were to move forward at my speed, about five yards apart and in complete silence, and that they pass my hand signals only, and if possible to work from tree to tree, or bush to bush. We started moving very slowly and silently stopping every few yards to search the ground and the trees. Having searched about three hundred yards I signalled a halt. We were just about to move on when there was a shot fired from forward and slightly to our right, it was a shot fired from a Japanese rifle, which unlike our ammunition gave a sound more like a "spat" rather than the crack. We changed direction and moved on very slowly, and after about fifty yards called another halt. I was just about to give the signal to move on when from a tree just five yards in front of us came a sneeze, followed by a second one. The man in the tree must have had his back to us and I could see farther down the slope that there was quite a large glade which he must have been covering.

All my men had heard the sneeze, I signalled them closer and we moved nearer the tree and searched with our eyes through the foliage. After a few minutes the man on the left put his thumb up and pointed to his rifle. I moved around to him and he whispered in my ear, "I can't see him but I can see his rifle." I then moved two men, one to the left and one the right, both with sten guns and instructed them that on my signal to spray the upper part of the tree where the rifle was. I raised an arm and brought it down sharply and the blasted the tree. There was not a sound from above but suddenly there were spots of blood dripping on the lower leaves. We waited about five minutes then cut the straps which were holding him in the tree and lowered him down. We searched his pockets and took his papers and identity disk, which would give the intelligence people something to work on.

I broke wireless silence and indicated that the job had been done, and the C.O. replied, "Well done John, thank your men." "Wilco and out." When we got back to Battalion H.Q. I reported to the C.O., he had apparently been watching my return with the carriers, he roasted me because I was not wearing my steel helmet.

The advance southwards became much slower, we were being shelled and attacked at night by large numbers of infantry who came and shouted cries for help and then fired tracer bullets into where our positions were, then when dawn came they had melted away into the hills, and the jungle that covered them. Towards the end of January, we were moving forward on a broad front clearing or "winkling", as it was called, the enemy out of hillocks, clumps of bamboo and small villages, as we went along.

I had been ordered to cover a 'C' Company platoon which had been given the task of clearing a small village surrounded by scrub and small trees. I had carriers on both flanks of the platoon moving at the speed the troops were going, when suddenly the leading section was fired on and went to ground, three men had been hit, the platoon commander gave me a target and the carriers mortared it and gave covering fire to the section as they moved forward.

Then came a major problem. We came to an area of paddy fields around the village and around the edge of the fields had been dug a large ditch which in the wet season was filled with water from the hills, and used to irrigate the paddy. It was as good as a tank trap. I radioed the platoon commander who was now about one hundred and fifty yards off the village and told him what had happened. He replied that he had lost another five men. Every carrier had a two-inch mortar and I asked him to stay low while the mortars concentrated on the targets and then we would give covering fire as the troops moved in. As they disappeared into the village we could hear the firing and the grenades exploding. The only firing was coming from the right hand side of the village and it was enemy fire.

The platoon commander reported that he had cleared his area, but was being fired on by two or three rifles on the right and "Could we help." As we left the carriers a number of ricochets were flying off the carrier, we split up into three groups of three, each group giving covering fire as we moved forward, when we got within ten yards of the bushes two Japanese got up and started to run, they were dispatched very quickly, we got into the bushes and followed a track towards the huts, I could hear my other two groups firing and grenades going off.

Suddenly we were confronted by two Japanese who were carrying rifles with fixed bayonets, the one nearest me charged forward and as he did so my batman Roberts opened up with his sten gun and shot them both, unfortunately the bayonet hit me in the right groin, and it was not until about ten minutes later it started to sting and bleed. I was lucky that it was not a major wound. In a few days it became infected and in a week, travelling by ambulance, river boat and tram, I was in hospital in Dacca. Almost immediately, I had the wound opened up and drained and spent my first day in a hospital bed for more than six weeks

The daily treatment was not very pleasant, long lengths of saturated dressing was fed into the wound and the next morning it was removed very slowly again to be replaced. There were seven other officers in the ward all with wounds of some sort, the most serious was the artillery officer who was standing by a twenty five pounder gun when the shell exploded in the breech and split his chest open and it was possible to see his lungs moving up and down as he breathed. They were all very congenial and there were times when we all had a laugh. It was on me one evening. After the lights were dimmed and it was time for sleep I couldn't get off to sleep, it was too hot in the mosquito net and I tossed and turned a few times. The rest of the men appeared to have gone to sleep. We had a very pretty Anglo-Indian nurse on night duty and she must have heard me moving, as she came along to my bed and whispered, "Is there anything I can do for you?" I replied "No thank you nurse." The men of course were awake and they cat-called and shouted "chicken" and other humorous but smutty inferences.

The wound was healing well and my bed was moved from the main ward on to the balcony or veranda and I was told to bare the wound to the sun for a short while each day. I was able to sit in a chair and go to the toilet on my own.

I was sitting there one day reading the "Indian Times" when a corporal came along and gave out mail, I had two airgraphs from my mother, a letter that came in two parts. The first told me news of my family and friends, and the second of a friend I used to play with as a lad. His name was Elwyn Lewis and he belonged to a very religious family. His father was the vicar of the Welsh chapel in Gelligroes between Wyllie and Pontllanfraith in

Islynn. He had two brothers and a sister. Veronwy had thick pebble glasses and a speech defect, but worked for the church. Herbert went to Aberystwyth Ecclesiastical University College and his sister did church work. When Herbert graduated he joined the Welsh Regiment as a padre, and was in southern India with his regiment. Elwyn had followed the family tradition and the last I heard of him he too, was in Ecclesiastical College in Aberystwyth.

Elwyn was engaged to a yong blonde lady from Oakdale, where Margaret and her family lived. My mother's letter went on to say "Keep an eye open for Elwyn Lewis, he is somewhere in India." She went on to say, Elwyn had made his young lady pregnant, and had to leave college. He was then called up for service and before he left for India, he married her. Then surprise, surprise, ten minutes after I read the letter, Elwyn came up the steps of the veranda. He was dressed in uniform with bush hat and his face was yellow. We greeted one another and I told him what my mother had said. He told me that he was on his way to join the Inniskelling Regiment in the Arakan but had been put off the train because he had jaundice. He asked for directions to the office and as he went off I told him that I would find out where he was and when possible I would visit him.

I visited him twice and kept a safe distance from him as he was in quarantine. I was sent to a recuperation centre for a week, near Calcutta, and bought myself a ring and a wedding ring for Margaret before I returned to hospital. When I got back Elwyn had been declared fit and had continued his journey to join his regiment. I too was declared fit and was ordered to return to my regiment. I went part of the way by rail then by military

105

transport to an officer posting centre in Chittagong. I was there for two days waiting for a river boat to Maungdau. While I was there I met Mickey Rooney who was a U.S. pilot ferrying equipment to China, and Melvyn Douglas, another actor who didn't say what he did.

There were two American reporters there, one a photographer and the other did the reports. They both had all their hair shaved off as they thought that they would be a long time away from civilisation. When I went to the dock to get on the river boat, they were being stretchered off a river boat that had just arrived from Maungdau. Both had been wounded, one in the shoulder and the other, five bullets in the upper thigh, which had gone right through. Apparently, travelling with them was a party of military police, who wore red tops to their hats. The Japanese pilot who strafed their boat must have thought that they were senior commanders because of their red hats. It was the end of the war for them.

I eventually rejoined my unit near a village called Ladu, there was daily activity on both sides, we were "winkling out", patrolling into the hills, being sniped at and shelled, but moving slowly towards Donbaik, which we learned was heavily defended from the central range to the sea. One day I was called to H.Q. and was ordered to provide a sentry post of one carrier plus driver, gunner and number two, plus a radio operator, to watch over a very narrow bridge which covered a chaung, to stop and search anyone moving over

I made a timetable so that the men did four hour stints in daylight and with an extra two men for eight hour shifts overnight. There were quite a few people arriving to cross every hour, mainly from the south to the north getting away from the shelling and bombing. We found natives who were in the pay of the Japanese, they had no pockets, but had Japanese money rolled into the top of their dhoti. When discovered they were handed over to the military police.

One morning a man came along carrying a pole on his shoulder and two baskets of rice, one on each end of the pole. He was searched and nothing was found, as he was about to move off I said to the sentry "Look in his rice." When the sentry stirred the rice we found two large belts of machinegun ammunition curled up in the baskets. He was handed over to the police. Quite often native Indians came along with their wives and daughters. The women were in purdah i.e. the hooded black cloak which only showed the person's eyes. The women were searched with as little embarrassment as possible, but on two occasions the persons under the cloak were male.

One evening as it was getting dark I had positioned the sentries, and placed my equipment by a large tree when I was called to the radio. My C.O. told me that he had received a report that a party of Japanese, all trained night fighters, armed with swords were coming north through the hills, and to report on any unusual happenings during the night. I "Wilcoed" and out, told the sentries and went back to my equipment and sat down, unfortunately on a bull frog, it made a dreadful noise and I don't know which jumped the higher, it or me. It left me with my heart racing like mad. About an hour later a red flare was set off by the Japanese in the hills about five miles away to the south east, to indicate to their troops they were in position. I took a bearing to the position of the flare and told H.Q. but heard nothing further about it.

Then came some very bad news. Men of the Inniskelling Fusiliers were coming in from the Mayu Ridge in very poor condition some without food and dressings for days, and very demoralised. Apparently the Inniskellings were part of a force fighting on the other side of the Mayu Ridge. Their commanding officer had commandeered every river craft he could to cross the Mayu River and attack the Japanese there. The left the western bank of the river before dawn thinking they had complete surprise, but in midstream they were attacked by machine guns and rifle fire and not one man survived the crossing.

When an opportunity arose, I made enquiries and ascertained that Lieutenant Elwyn Lewis was posted "Missing, Believed Killed", after that incident. More of that later.

The news from Donbaik was not good, tanks were brought in to support the infantry and during the attacks were bogged down with the muddy ground, and quickly destroyed. The pockets of Japanese had disappeared and it was assumed they had gone into the bunkers and Donbaik.

We were now about three miles from Donbaik and the men were holed up near the gun batteries. We knew that there was some activity going on when the big guns fired a lengthy barrage, it was to deal with an attack or counter-attack. On, or about the 8th March the C.O. took the company commanders and me forward to within 150 yards of the British positions, we met the intelligence officer of the Indian Regiment which was holding the line, and he took us up a tall hillock from which they had driven the Japanese, and which looked down on the Chaung and open ground before the bunkers which were well camouflaged and hard to see. Apparently there were two bunkers opposite us, they were named Sugar 5 and Sugar 4. What was frightening about this picture, was that there were many bodies lying in front of the bunkers. There were also bodies lying on top of the bunkers. The intelligence officer told us that there were also bunkers behind those and also gunpits which stretched to the beach which was to our right.

Up to that day, every attack that had been made on the Japanese positions had been repulsed, with a large loss of men both killed and wounded. Many patrols were sent out to try and discover any weak spots they might have in their defensive positions but some came back with wounds, others didn't return at all. On 10th March 1943, the Royal Welch Fusiliers 1st Battalion took over the positions opposite Sugar 5 and 4, with the 2nd Durham Light Infantry on our left flank. In the rear was a battalion of the Royal Scots.

When the brigadier of 6th Brigade saw the carnage surrounding the Japanese positions he prepared a plan of attack completely different from previous plans which had failed. Colonel Cavendish submitted the plan to the High Command which recommended that no barrage be laid down before the attack, that the British move in silently just before dawn. Whilst waiting for a reply to the new proposal we and the D.L.I. were holding meetings to discuss the pending attack making sure that arms and ammunition and stretcher bearers were ready. Lt. Colonel Humphrey Williams called the officers not on

109

immediate duty to a conference just to the rear of the position. Colonel Williams had just started his meeting and we were perched on the edge of what looked like a bomb crater, when suddenly there was a "whoosh" followed by an explosion during which my friend Douglas Lyman (Major) was hit in the back by a piece of shrapnel, and rolled over. We called "stretcher bearers," and he was carried off to the R.A.P. (Regimental Aid Post).

The doctor had dressed the wound, given him a morphine injection and was waiting for an ambulance when I went to see Douglas. He gave me his home address so that if I made it through the campaign I knew where I could find him. That was on the 12th March, 1943.

In the meantime a reply came from Delhi "The change of plan was not accepted, the bunkers were to be taken by the bayonet." Early on the 16th March, 1943 a very heavy barrage was put down on the bunkers. As the barrage lifted every one cheered but didn't move. On the 17th March the same happened again. On the 18th March at 5.00 a.m. the barrage lifted and the attack was for real. I was with the reserve unit.

All hell was let loose, many men reached the top of the bunkers which were shelled and mortared by the Japanese. We then received a message from the C.O. to the effect that many men of D Company were on top of the bunker and that a company of the Royal Scots were coming through us to try and get D Company out. In addition, the C.O. Col. Humphrey Williams, spoke in Welsh using a loud hailer to D Company telling them about the Royal Scots coming and describing the best routes to use to rejoin the regiment. The Scots attempt to bring D Company in as they were subjected to heavy mortar and shellfire was not successful.

A few returned, some wounded but no officers. Late that afternoon, Col. Williams sent for me and told me that he felt there could be a counter-attack made by the Japanese during the night and that he wanted me to go to the rear of our positions, on a rocky outcrop with two of my men. To take a two-inch mortar and sufficient parachute flares to last all night and at irregular intervals fire the flares over the bunkers, and should I see any movement which would indicate a counter-attack to fire red flares. At the same time he had arranged with the gunners to lay fire down on the top of the bunkers. This caused me more concern than the Japanese. One gun which was about five miles away was stripping the driving bands off the shells. As the shells were falling about fifty yards in front of us you could hear them wobbling as they came over, and closely followed by pieces of broken control bands, which were too close for comfort.

At midday on 19th March, 1943 the British positions opposite the bunkers were little changed from that of forty-eight hours previously, but the Royal Welch had lost upwards of one-hundred-and-fifty men missing believed killed, and thirteen officers.

Nothing seemed to go as planned, the R.A.F. were to have bombed the bunkers and the southern side of the chaung, but bombed the village of Donbaik, which was a mile-and-a-half away from the target.

By the 20th March, 1943 the bodies on the bunkers and in the chaung area had turned black and burst, and the stench of putrefying flesh made it difficult to breathe. I and some of my men felt sick what made things worse were the flies which got everywhere. Not long after the attack we were moved back from the area and the bodies were blown away by the gunners.

After this the Japanese attacked the D.L.I. who were on the left flank and tried to circle around the brigade and pin them down. I was told to put the carriers in defensive spots around the wood near where we were and to cover the companies as they retreated from forward positions. As they came out the Royal Scots took over. By midday the wood was a fortress, machinegun posts had been set up, and troops who had occupied the woods earlier in the campaign had dug mortar pits and slit trenches. It must have been an Indian native regiment because when the sandbags in the parapets were tidied up seven-pound tins of bully beef had been built into the structure. (Hindus worship the cow.) It went down very well.

In the middle of the afternoon I said to Roberts my batman, have a look around and find me a hole were I can put my equipment and have a sleep. He found a place for me, it was shaped like a grave and about two foot deep. I took my equipment off and arranged my pack like a pillow. I lay down, and as I did so looked at the tree behind me. I took a second look, it was full of bullet holes. I realised that it was on a fixed line and was not safe to be near. I called Roberts, and he moved me to a spot where the tree behind the position was clear. A short while afterwards a quartermaster sergeant came along with two men carrying dixies (food containers).

"Grub up" they called, and moved towards us on a little path between the trees. Moments after they arrived there was the sound of a shell, it exploded, and billowed smoke. I shouted, get under cover and keep your heads down. It showed where the shell had landed, they then ranged their guns on to the area where the smoke came from.

Sure enough, the next one was high explosive. They fired about six shells and then stopped. The next call was for "stretcher bearers". I got up and went to where the call came from and found that the quartermaster sergeant had dived into the hole that I had vacated. A shell had burst on the tree with the bullet holes, and had smashed his steel helmet.

A few days later we came under heavy machinegun fire from a clump of bamboo about 500 yards away. The C.O. called on the artillery for concentrated fire on the clump and it was shelled for about ten minutes. As the shelling lifted I took three carriers with three riflemen in each, one on the left of the trees, one on the right and mine to the centre firing bren guns as we went. There was no return fire and as we got to the trees we found six dead Japanese, and nearby a heavy machinegun and the two crew dead. We spread out and searched the area and found a Japanese soldier without rifle or steel helmet, sitting on the ground and it was fairly obvious that he was very shell-shocked. He was the first prisoner we had taken, and as we had heard that when taken prisoner they tried to kill themselves, and their captors, we searched him and found nothing. His hands were bound behind his back and we lifted him into the carrier and took him back to Battalion H.Q.

When the C.O. saw him, he said "I don't want him, what can I do with him?" Take him to the provost staff and he explained that they were on the other side of the wood we were in. By now it was getting dark and I set off with the Jap and a rifleman. As well as the darkness it was possible to smell smoke from grass and undergrowth which had caught fire during the shelling. Without warning I felt myself dropping still clutching the Jap's jacket by the neckband. We hit the ground feet first and immediately I called the rifleman he said "Where are you?" I replied that I think we have dropped into a chaung. I turned around and felt the bank then reached up and said go carefully it is a drop about six feet. It was not very wide and we found a place where we got the prisoner up reasonably easy. Not long afterwards we were challenged and handed the prisoner over to the provost. I asked them to radio my operator and to say I would return at first light.

Just before dawn they gave me a mug of tea and as I was drinking it I realised that the ring, which was normally on the little finger of my left hand was missing. I told the rifleman who was with me that we would try and retrace our route of the previous night, and try and find it. We eventually reached the chaung which was very rocky and uneven and told him where the Jap and I had landed there was a soft spot which felt like sand. We followed the chaung along and suddenly came to two sets of feet marks in the only sandy patch for at least a 100 yards. And there sitting on the sandbank was my ring.

It was fortunate that things were very quiet, the Japanese must have been concentrating on our left flank where the Durham Light Infantry (D.L.I.) were, as we

114

could hear the sound of shelling and machineguns. I say it was fortunate as some men who were digging a gun pit near a clump of bushes, looked into the bushes and found three or four large cardboard cartons, which had been hidden by someone. They opened them and discovered they were packed with tins of raspberries in fruit juice, and tins of evaporated milk. After bully and army biscuits ad infinitum, this was like a birthday party until three or four hours afterwards, when men were seen heading for the latrines and woods. They were glad to get back to bully and biscuits.

A short while later we moved north towards Indin for about ten miles, into bandit country. The battalion was in a long straggly wood midway between the sea and the wooded mountains, which were about five miles away, and on top of which the Japs had at least one piece of artillery. I had been with my men on a standing patrol about two hundred yards from where a jungle path came down from the hill side. Some of my men were positioned near the path watching for Japanese scouts. We had not had a decent night's sleep for three days and when the brigade carrier officer Captain Reggie Parrish came to visit, I told him that my men were very tired and suggested that he relieve us for twenty four hours. He agreed, and at midday the D.L.I. carrier officer came along and took over our positions. As a joke I said to him "If you get bored you can listen to Tokyo Rose." I withdrew my carriers to join the battalion and we spent the rest of the afternoon cleaning weapons.

The sewing machine spotter plane came over in the afternoon, but again, it was not fired on and I wondered why, as it was obvious we had been seen. This was proven just before dawn as we were shelled from the hills. After the shelling and bully soup I told my men to make the most of the time and get some sleep in. I doubt whether they did, like myself, I could not sleep, and I went over to a group of people who I guessed from the noises were loading up mules. There were nine mules so I assumed there were nine muleteers. I asked where they were going, and the reply was "They are taking food and ammunition to a company for the Royal Scots." They moved off eventually and I thought to myself, that is one job I would not like to do, as they disappeared into the darkness.

The next day a Captain Rissik of the D.L.I. was sent forward with a platoon of the Special Service company and a section of carriers, and they stopped and interrogated a couple of Indian soldiers from a mule company, fleeing from an attack which the Japanese made on a bridge over a chaung, which the Royal Scots had been guarding. Captain Rissik established that the Japanese were in about company strength. He moved cautiously forward with his men and found the remains of the mule company. There were about six dead mules, and the bodies of fourteen dead men. All had at least half-a-dozen bayonet wounds and some were badly slashed with sword cuts. There was one man barely alive, and he died later.

A few days later I had to attend a briefing as we were due to withdraw still further, when the D.L.I. carrier officer came along and was introduced to me, it was not the fellow I had handed over to a few days previously, with the joke about Tokyo Rose. He replied that the carrier officer was sitting on the ground, with his back to his carrier, listening to the radio and he was shot by a sniper from the jungle. Things were getting really bad, we were being attacked from the south and from the hills which overlooked us. Some evenings when the moon came up the hills echoed with the sound of bren and rifle fire, the bursting of mortar bombs and grenades and the cries of the attackers and the attacked. The Japanese came in shouting "Don't shoot we are Royal Scots. Don't shoot." They were greeted with a blaze of fire and the bayonet. They then melted away into the jungle on the hills leaving their dead.

One incident I will never forget. I needed to use the toilet, in this instance, the latrine. When I got there the pole was fully occupied, in addition there was no toilet paper. I remembered that on the way to Battalion H.Q. which was about a hundred-and-fifty yards away there was a banyan tree which came down like an open umbrella and the leaves touched the ground so that the trunk was hidden. I walked to it, and on the way I picked some soft foliage like ferns, to take the place of toilet paper. Over a long period, that tree and others nearby had dropped a carpet of leaves which rustled and crunched underfoot. I arrived at the tree, lifted the branches and went under, and there was quite a large space underneath. I took my equipment off and placed it well away from me with my sten gun. I was doing what I had to do when I heard a rustle of leaves outside, then another footstep and yet another. The perspiration was dripping off my forehead and my nose and I thought to myself "You're dead." The footsteps stopped near the fringe of the trees, and I froze. The leaves rustled and suddenly a large brown snake pushed it's head between the leaves. Very quickly I removed a piece of parachute silk I had around my neck and waved it at the snake, and it slithered off. I felt as though I had gone very pale.

Everyone carries a piece of yellow parachute silk which was laid out in a clearing for the pilots who were carrying food, to know when to drop their parachutes.

We were about five miles out of Indin, ahead of us a company of the Royal Scots had been cut off and the Japs had circled to the north of 6th Brigade which meant that the withdrawal of the brigade had been halted. My commanding officer sent for me and told me to report to Captain Duffy Rees who was a Royal Welshman, and intelligence officer to the Brigadier. When I met Captain Rees he told me that the brigadier was moving his headquarters and I was, with my men, to build a sandbagged strongpoint for the Brigadier and his staff to the west of the Royal Welsh left flank. He showed me where it was to be sited and it was completed and occupied in one day. Colonel Williams suggested I leave a bren gun carrier, with a driver, for the use of the Brigadier. I did so and allotted Fusilier (Lazy) Lawrence as his driver.

About an hour before it got dark I was informed that the Royal Welch were to attack the hill in front, which was held by the Japs, that I, with the carriers, were to follow the attack and give support when necessary. A short while after learning this we came under very heavy machinegun fire from the hill which was to be attacked next day, and shelling from the high ground to the right. This lasted about half-an-hour, then the firing stopped, and it was difficult to see in the darkness.

In the early hours of the morning Fusilier Lawrence, closely followed by Captain Duffy Rees, who had been slightly wounded, came into our lines. Captain Rees described how under the machine gunning and shelling a Japanese raiding party had overrun the Brigadier's sandbagged position, and had taken away Brigadier Cavendish and his staff. Fusilier Lawrence had been asleep in his carrier, both he and Duffy Rees had got away in the confusion.

The Japanese had wrecked the radio and telephone equipment which left the brigade isolated from Colonel Hopkins who was now brigade commander, as Brigadier Cavendish had been captured, and the gunners were also isolated from their units. As a result the attack due to be made by the R.W.F. was postponed.

At first light the next morning I took two volunteers in a bren gun carrier through the Japanese lines and on to the edge of the beach, under erratic shell and rifle fire and headed north. After about two miles I first met a large artillery gun which they were going to use on me if I had been Japanese. Colonel Hopkins was there, and I gave him details of what had happened overnight. He gave me and my men something to eat, and also new wavelengths for the use of 6th Brigade communications. I then set off with the information.

I stopped halfway and used my binoculars to search the landscape to the north of where the attack was due to be made and saw Japanese soldiers, some in uniform and others dressed as Indians. I returned to Colonel Williams with the new wavelengths, the gunners were informed and new plans for the attack drawn up. The attack started about four o'clock, and by five was completed and was a success. Troops returning from the hill reported that there were many dead Japanese on and behind the hill but no sign of Brigadier Cavendish or his staff. The carriers of the D.L.I. and R.W. Fusiliers later destroyed the sandbagged strongpoint and the Japanese in it. Both my men, Fusiliers T. Radcliffe and J. Brown were awarded the M.M. Both were stretcher bearers at Kohima, where Tommy Radcliffe was killed.

The following day the brigade commander ordered the D.L.I. and the Royal Welch to attack the Japanese to relieve the Royal Scots who had had a hammering during the night. The daylight revealed the Japanese, walking in the open plain, attempting to find cover among bamboo clumps and scattered huts. British mortars and artillery were turned on them and the bren guns and riflemen were shooting them down by scores. If they remained in the shelter of the huts and trees they were blown to pieces by the 25-pounders. Many of them ran towards us screaming as they left their cover, and were mown down. When the firing eventually stopped the bren gun that my No.1 had been firing was so hot you could smell it but not touch it. It was the only bright moment in the Arakan Campaign. For once the Japanese had been well and truly thrashed.

During the day Colonel B. Hopkins had made plans for the brigade to withdraw north to Kyaukpandu that afternoon, starting at 1300 hours. Meanwhile, the slaughter of the Japanese in the Indin area went on, the twenty-five-pounders and mortars shelling and bombing until all the men and vehicles had withdrawn to the beach. The brigade carriers covered the withdrawal and then escorted the men on to the beach. I have never seen anything like it before. The long column of soldiers and vehicles moved along the beach to the north and safety. As far as I am aware, not a man was lost in the withdrawal. I towed one ambulance out of the sand and I lost one bren gun carrier which dug itself further into the sand as we tried to tow it out. A grenade was exploded in its engine and regretfully it was left on the beach, and may still be there. By three o'clock in the afternoon the operation was successfully completed.

This campaign was controlled by commanders in Delhi, and the one who ordered that the bunkers Sugar 4 and 5 should be taken by the bayonet should have been certified as insane. When General Bill Slim arrived on the scene, like a breath of fresh air, he said "That the Battle of Donbaik should never have taken place." 6th Brigade sustained 2500 battle casualties which were far outnumbered by the sick, mainly from malaria.

We had left Kyaukpandu and Maungdau behind and there was an unfortunate incident which could have happened either at Bawle Bazaar, or Cox's Bazaar, I can't remember. I had supplied a working party with a corporal in charge, to hollow out and enlarge a cave which was to house ammunition, grenades, mortar bombs etcetera, and which would then be sealed.

The rest of my men were cleaning and servicing carriers, mortars and brens when there was an explosion followed by a much bigger one. We ran to where the ammunition was being loaded into the cave, and found that the corporal had been killed and two men seriously wounded. It was difficult to find out how or what caused the initial explosion. We were very deeply upset as the three men were very good soldiers and had fought stoically throughout the campaign. A few days later the two men died from their injuries and I had the unhappy task of writing to their next of kin. The rest of the ammunition was taken to a dried up river bed and blown up.

It took us about a month to reach Chittagong, from where we started the long journey to Bombay using barges to cross the Brahmaputra and Ganges rivers, and then by train. Having reached Bombay we continued our journey by road via Poona and then Ahmednagar.

We were greeted by the C.O. who gave us a week to clean and check vehicles, guns and other arms which were oiled and put into store. Then we were taken to a hill station on the Deccan, Marble Shwar, which had a climate much like a good English summer, and we had anti-malarial treatment for about ten days. We were living in Bell tents which were fitted with camp beds. The first day's treatment was ten quinine tablets. Second day nine tablets and so on. By the time we had finished the treatment, our eyeballs and skin were yellow, and we all felt sick.

The area where we were had quite a lot of trees but there were tracks which led into open areas where there were native huts and usually chickens around and the men bartered for eggs. They came back one day form a walk and asked me permission to keep a pig. One of the men had worked for 'Mac Fisheries' in peacetime and he said he would look after it, and fatten it up for Christmas. Just to be safe I mentioned the pig to the adjutant and he said "Why not?" So the men built a pen with branches and with walls about five feet high and between them they agreed a price and installed the pig. They fed the pig with some of their rations and the cooks gave them bits from the kitchen. It augured well for Christmas.

One morning there was a shout from nearby "The pig is out" and men came from everywhere and disappeared after the pig. They came back in ones and twos telling the story that it had outrun them. The man who saw it escape said "I was just going to give it a few crumbs and as I got near to the pen it cleared the top like a bloody steeple chaser." I was telling the story of the pig to a chap I had met a few times I the Marble Shwar Officer's Club. He said every regiment that has been here for blanket treatment has bought that pig, and it always gets away.

After a restful period and our colour had returned to normal we were taken back to Ahmednagar, and new men and officers arrived to replace those who had died or been wounded. Shortly after returning from Marble Shwar we were told that the second battalion which had been in Shanghai before the war, and had then moved on from there to Malta and Gibraltar had arrived in India and were stationed in Poona. Their commanding officer Lt. Col. Gwydur-Jones had invited us to go to Poona to play rugby and soccer against their teams, the officers to dine together, other ranks and N.C.O.s to get together and have a good time. There had always been rivalry between the two battalions this became very marked when the games started. I played rugby for the battalion and the army in peacetime, and I thought that we might get beaten as we had lost some of our best players.

However there were some good players in our new intake and we stormed ahead. There was quite a lot of bad temper and fouling but by half-time we were ten points in the lead. During the interval their captain had complained to the referee that the ground was too hard and that three of his side had been lost because of this. The game was abandoned.

The following day we beat them at soccer. On the Friday following, a concert party entertained everyone in the large marquee and before the show and afterwards quite a lot of beer was consumed and there were clashes after lights out. On the Saturday the officers were dining together and the non-commissioned officers had their own function. Before dinner Douglas Lyman and I went into their mess and had a few beers before we were called into the dining room. One wall of the room was stacked with the 2nd Battalion silver and trophies which they had brought from England with them. The meal was sumptuous but I couldn't eat anything, I kept thinking of the folk at home and rationing.

After dinner we retired to the mess for coffee and liqueurs and we stood or sat in groups with our regiments and not mixing as we should. After the coffee was finished our C.O. Lt. Col. Humphrey Williams went to the piano and he played a classical piece of music which ended with applause. He then played a few opening bars and started to sing.

"I wish I was a fascinating bitch,

I would never be poor, I'd always be rich,

I'd live in a house with a little red light,

I would sleep all day and work all night,

Oh, I wish…"

And we from the 1st Battalion joined in the last line. It went very quiet and an officer from the 2nd Battalion stood up and said to the room "That was disgusting." Then there was chaos.

A lieutenant from the 2nd Battalion stood up and punched at Douglas. I picked up a very large receptacle containing water and flowers from the table near us and put it over his head. Fortunately someone switched the lights out and the riotous behaviour stopped. During the night guy ropes on tents were taken off the pegs and the tents collapsed, and the move continued until after midnight.

The battalion returned to Ahmednagar the following day very much under a cloud. During the fracas Lt. Col. Gwydur Jones lost his stick, which was about five feet high and had been cut into a 'Y' shape at the top. His thumb fitted into the 'Y' and thus, he called it his 'Y' stick. The stick was found about a week later in the Sergeant's Mess in Ahmednagar and returned to Lt. Col. Gwydur Jones in Poona.

Then followed a period when all personnel could go on leave. I chose to go to Marble Shwar as I had been invited to stay with David and Jean Chambers, and their two boys. David was tax collector for the Bombay Province. He lived in a large government bungalow, and his duties included ensuring that all taxes were paid and necessitated a great deal of travelling in the province. After I had been with them for a week and had been treated royally, with picnics and riding, plus tennis, David announced that he was off on his travels, and I felt that as he was leaving it would be best that I did to. Both he and Jean insisted that I stay my leave out, but fate took a hand and I went down with malaria. I was taken by ambulance to the Military Hospital at Ahmednagar and didn't see them again. I did however write to thank them for my holiday. Apparently Jean and the boys had visited me in hospital, but I didn't remember it.

When the Battalion had arrived back in Ahmednagar morale was good. We had been taught a lesson by the Japs in the Arakan but as we left we had thrashed them, captured diaries showed that one Japanese regiment had been reduced to eighty me from an original thousand. When I had been in hospital two events had taken place which had upset every one. Admiral Lord Louis Mountbatten had been to Ahmednagar to present decorations and medals to people who had been awarded them for bravery in action. Before this had been arranged Lt. Col Humphrey Williams, our C.O. had been awarded a D.S.O. (Distinguished Service Order) and was being sent back to England to command a battalion of the Royal Welsh Fusiliers, which would be landing in France on D. Day.

He had been replaced by a Lieutenant Colonel Braithwaite, whom we had known as a Captain Braithwaite in Blackdown, pre-war. Then, he was known as "Braggas", and was unpopular, being arrogant and nasty tempered. He had organised the presentation and had arranged for the band of the 2nd Battalion from Poona to play at the presentation even though our band had lost a few men in action, there were enough to play for the occasion, or to join up with the other band. They were completely ignored. Our adjutant Captain Martin Lloyd Davis who had served with Humphrey Williams had been replaced by another officer and Major Johnny Vaughan became second-in-command.

The morale of both officers and men did a nosedive. The replacement officers in the mess did not know Braithwaite and Vaughan as we did, and officers who knew them and were outspoken in the mess about them were posted away. On a wireless exercise, during a lull in the procedures, two company commanders made derogatory remarks about the C.O. which he heard. The exercise was terminated and the two officers were posted away the next day. Some days later, after this incident the C.O. sent for me. On the way to H.Q. I really thought I was going the same way. I had not spoken to anyone about Colonel Braithwaite or the new officers, though I didn't like him or the new second-in-command, whom I had also known pre-war. When I got to the office I reported to Major Johnny Vaughan and he informed the C.O. I was there.

I was invited in, I saluted, and I was offered a chair. I sat down, and he C.O. said "I understand that you've been doing a captain's job for the last few months." I replied "Yes, sir." And then he said, "Well done, when you leave here you may put another pip up. You are Captain Bennett now." I thanked him, saluted and left. He knew me as an old Royal Welsh man and I had the feeling that he was trying to buy my loyalty. I was however very pleased with the promotion. About a month later the 2nd British Division which involved the 4th, 5th and 6th Brigades were moved down to Belgaun which is on the Goanese border for jungle training, which was particularly for the new men and officers who had replaced the men killed or wounded in the Arakan.

The monsoon had recently ended, the jungle was green and cool, pleasant to work in. After about a week we had a rest day and my friend Douglas and I went for a walk on one of the tracks near where we were bivouacked. We had travelled about a mile when we came to a railway line which we followed and eventually came to a station. Where the line carried on from the station, there was a barrier and we realised then that on

127

the other side was Goa, which was governed by the Portugese. We went into the station and had a couple of beers and spent some time talking to the member of staff on duty there. He told us that two trains a day went into Goa, and returned, one in the afternoon, and the other in the evening. Also, that if we needed it, the driver and fireman would bring back wine or spirits hidden under the coal, and they needed the money to take into Goa to buy the goods. We declined. We also learned that there was a dance in the railway hall on Saturday nights and that the Davis girls would by there and Mrs. MacTavish with her family.

On Saturday Douglas and I set off with torches, heading for the dance wearing ammunition boots. When we got there we found that there were more soldiers there than there were ladies, and that Mr. Davis and Mr. MacTavish had married local girls some fifty years ago.

And then came the news that the Japanese had made a flanking movement through the mountains, and that they were very close to the border of India. The Second British Division were ordered to return and prepare for war. I was ordered to get the carriers back to Ahmednagar. On our arrival at Ahmednagar I reported to the C.O., who gave me brief details of what had happened, and he gave me forty-eight hours in which to prepare men and vehicles for the journey to Assam. All weapons had to be cleaned, oiled and crated and all types of ammunition stored in place. Having done this before and having been trained in the procedures this was completed in less than a day.

Whilst this was going on I attended a briefing where I learned more about the situation. I was issued with maps which would take me across India and a list which gave details of places where I could get rations, first aid and petrol. Also, staging areas when the crews could get a bath and change of clothing. Before our departure I was able to talk to the men to tell them as much as I could. I had two dispatch riders with me, one had to be leading the convoy the other to travel at the rear, behind the ordnance vehicle, which carries the mechanics and spares. Early on this day we left Ahmednagar and our route ran through Wardha, Nagpur, Rajpur, Ranchi, Sylhet, Shillong and ultimately Dimapur. Most of the country was beautiful, there were times when we travelled for miles only seeing a child minding a herd of goats or bullock carts heading for the towns. We passed estates with high walls surrounding the local Rajah's palace where there were peacocks strutting around and occasional glimpses of beautiful buildings set in trees and well-tended lawns. We had been travelling about three days and at nights, sleeping either in the carriages or wrapped in a blanket on the ground. Also, our diet was not very interesting, most of our food was tinned. Then I had, what I thought, a good idea. We were preparing to find a suitable place to stop for the night when we passed a large lake which had a number of big, tall, white long legged birds standing in the water. About a half a mile further along the road there was a small village. We stopped and I sent two men, one of them had worked in Mac Fisheries before the war, back to the lake to acquire two birds. Another corporal I dispatched to the village to buy unions and whatever vegetables he could get and sufficient rice to feed everyone.

There were dixies in the van which we used to make tea, but this time it was to be casseroled bird. The Mac Fisheries man was in charge of the operation and other men were detailed to help. In the meantime, those not cooking were washing and relaxing whilst waiting for the meal. Then came the call "Grub up. Come and get it." The men turned up with their mess tines and knives and forks, and lined up. The dixies were brought along, lids taken off, ladles stirred the contents, and when the meat and vegetables were put into mess tins the meat was bright orange, and no one would eat it. We returned to the bully beef again.

After ten days travelling we arrived at a staging camp, very dusty and tired, it had been very hot. As usual the vehicles were serviced and made ready for the next part of the journey. Some of them needed their tracks adjusted, as with the travelling they stretched, and it affected the steering. When all was completed my sergeant reported that he had been told there was a river nearby and there were towels that the men could use and that part of the river had been roped off where the men could swim. As there was about two hours before their meal, could they swim? I agreed and arranged for two N.C.O.s who didn't wish to swim, to ensure that everything that took place was safe. To count the number of heads that went and make sure they had the same number on return.

What the sergeant was not told was that further up stream on the banks of the river were burning Ghals, where people burnt the corpses of relatives who had died. Sometimes, the poor who couldn't afford the fire just cast the bodies into the river, and occasionally these could be seen. As a result the men came back clutching their clothes and towels demanding disinfectant, special soap and scrubbing brushes. They were all able to shower before their meal and no-one suffered from anything that may have been in the river.

Eventually we arrived at the most important stop of our journey to Assam. It was the city of Ranchi which is the capital of Bihar Province, and was the rear echelon of the Royal Welch Fusiliers. It was the centre where all information regarding the activities of men and officers of the Regiment were collated, recorded and where information was transferred to Army Records and eventually to the War Office. One of the staff there was an old friend of mine and to gain information about the whereabouts of the Regiment I sought for my friend Jerry Vaux and soon found him. He told me that fighting was taking place at Jotsoma about two miles from Kohima which was under siege. Some casualties had been reported but as he had been unable to get radio contact with the Regiment, he did not know exactly where they were. But he knew that there were wounded at Dimapur and Sylhet.

After a two day rest period at Ranchi I set off with the carriers for Sylhet. We had to change frequently from narrow gauge railways to broad gauge rate then vice versa when crossing tributaries of the Ganges, which held us up at times, and then we started to leave the plains and to climb mountains. The air became fresher and at nights quite chilly and the nature of the geography changed from lush broad leafed trees to sparse clumps of conifers and other fir trees. On arrival at Sylhet I reported to the garrison officer and was allotted temporary billets for me and the men. After I had seen that they had been fed, I then inquired about casualties and the hospital. The garrison commander gave me his car and driver for the evening and I was taken to the hospital. I was quite surprised to find that the nurses were dressed in a sort of Welsh costume.

I reported to the matron officer and explained why I was there and was then taken to a ward where I believe that the man in bed was Lieutenant H.A. Curtis of my regiment. He had been on a patrol with two other men when a Japanese officer stepped out from behind a tree and aimed at him with a samurai sword. The men with Lt. Curtis shot the Japanese officer but the sword had hit Curtis across the upper arm and made a deep cut. He did not know where the Regiment was since his admission to hospital. I wished him well and left him. In another ward I spoke to a fusilier who had been wounded in the legs at Jatsoma. He told me that there had been heavy fighting there and that Lt. John Rostron had been killed by a sniper. He also said that the Durham Light Infantry were attacking Garrison Hill and trying to open the road to relieve the siege. I decided then to leave the next day for Shillong and then Dimapur.

When I arrived at Shillong I found out that 6th Brigade which included the Royal Welch, were close to Kohima and that the Durham Light Infantry had broken through the Japanese lines in places and that the attacks were continuing. By the time I reached Dimapur the siege of Kohima had been lifted, the Durhams had been relieved by the Royal Welch who were now in position on Garrison Hill. However the position was such that air drops of food, ammunition and medical supplies were continuing and ambulances were ferrying the wounded and sick to hospital in Dimapur.

It was amazing to think that not long before the whole 2nd Division was on jungle training in Belgaum 1500 miles away, and they were now fighting the Japanese in Assam.

When I arrived with the carriers and their crews in Dimapur, I contacted 6th Brigade rear echelon and was requested to hand over the carriers to the Ordinance Corps after removing all weaponry and ammunition. We were then allotted tents in a staging area where all the clothing we carried was fumigated whilst everyone had a haircut and shower. We then had a substantial mean and were allowed to rest for twenty-four hours. At midday the next day I had been ordered to parade the men ready for transfer to Kohima. On the parade firearms were checked by a team of Royal Ordinance men and fifty rounds of ammunition was given to each man in bandoleers or magazines according to the weapon he was carrying. I handed my revolver over and was issued with a sten gun. In addition each man carried an empty sandbag which before leaving was half-filled with rations. We were then loaded into troop carrying vehicles in the late afternoon and started our journey up the mountain roads to Kohima.

It was a very narrow road and we had to pull into 'passing points' to allow ambulancemen and other military vehicles to pass. Also on the road we were passing the odd ammunition boot and pairs of boots in some cases and when we stopped at one point I asked the driver about them. He told me that some of the Indian regiments that had marched up the road preferred to walk barefooted and just cast their army boots away.

When we arrived at Kohima we were stopped by sentries where there were two tanks blocking the road. We were directed to sit in a particular area until an officer came to see us. It was early evening and being 15000ft up quite chilly. Also all around, no matter where you sat was the sickening smell of dead bodies. We waited about twenty minutes and I then heard a familiar voice asking for Captain Bennett. It was Johnny Owens second-in-command of the Battalion. He had been commissioned in the field as I had been. He said "Sorry to have left you sitting for a while, but it's better to move around in the dark as there are snipers about." Before the Regiment went to the borders of Goa for jungle training we had been fighting down the west coast of Burma and had become familiar with the names of the towns and villages there. But when we were ordered to get to Kohima quickly no one apart from the senior officers had any idea where Kohima was.

After returning from the jungle training in Goa, and whilst the men were preparing vehicles for the journey across India from Ahmednagar to Calcutta, and the loading of arms and ammunition was preceeding, I attended a briefing where I learned where Kohima was and how important it was to get there quickly. Kohima is a small hill town in N.E. Assam sitting astride a narrow road which meanders through and around a mountainous area and was 5000ft above sea level. Kohima was an important hill station 15000 feet above sea level on the only road that led from the major British supply depot at Dimapur to Imphal, another British Indian outpost.

Assam and especially the Naga Hills is probably the wettest place on earth and the jungle clad mountains can only be described as hellish. Men and animals are tormented by saw flies, ticks, mosquitoes and leeches. Dengue, Scrub Typhus, Malaria and Cholera are endemic to the area. Prior to 1941 Japan had been at

134

war with China but on 7th December 1941 the Japanese bombed Pearl Harbour and America entered the war against Japan, Italy and Germany. Meanwhile, the Japanese increased their attacks on South East Asia which was completely unprepared and by 7th March 1942, Singapore had fallen to them, and Rangoon was also captured, and Mandalay overrun. There was a great exodus of the British from Burma into India. The threat then was to India itself, and the first defensive position was Kohima.

The ground over which the battle for Kohima was fought is difficult to imagine. The town was the administrative centre of Nagaland and had a military supply depot, hospital and staging post, about a third of the way between Dimapur and Imphal, and the names of the features were to become familiar to thousands of British, Gurkha and Indian soldiers.

The road from Dimapur climbed in a curve around the 53rd Indian General Hospital (I.G.H.) spur, and after passing the Deputy Commissioners (D.C.s) Bungalow, it turned in a sharp hairpin. From the D.C.'s Bungalow the road ran south past Garrison Hill, the Kuki Picket, Field Supply Depot (F.D.S), Detail Issue (D.I.) Hill, Jail Hill and General Purpose Transport (G.P.T.) Ridge. There was also a Field Bakery, a Transport Company, and an Ordnance Store. There were no prepared defensive positions, and no barbed wire.

In mid-March the only troops in the Kohima area were Assam Rifles and Assam Regiment, then General Slim flew the 5th Indian Division into Dimapur and the 161st Indian Brigade were moved down the road to Kohima. The rest of the reinforcements and the Brigade Artillery were placed two miles away in Jotsoma. On the evening of 5th/6th April, 1944, the attacks started and went on daily and at night until 8th April. On the 9th April the defendants of the Bungalow area were forced back to the tennis court.

This area was the scene of some of the hardest, closest and grimmest fighting. In the end the attacks were beaten off with the help of remarkably accurate fire from the artillery at Josoma ridge. The Garrison was still isolated as the Japanese held the road to Jotsoma and Dimapur, supplies were dropped by air to the defenders.

On the 14th April, 1944, the 2nd British Division arrived at Dimapur from the 1500 mile flight which had brought them from the border of Goa. On the morning of 18th April British artillery opened up against the Japanese positions. The Durham Light Infantry and Royal Welch Fusiliers of 6th Brigade, 2nd British Division plus tanks from 33 Corps pushed into an area of Garrison Hill and forced the Japanese from their positions. The road to Dimapur had been opened and the siege lifted.

We gathered around Major Owens. He then shone a very small light on the clip board he carried and I assumed it was a list of the names of the men that had travelled with me in the carriers, which I had handed in our arrival at Dimapur. He said "John, you are to join 'B' Company as second-in-command." Some of the men were to join A, B, C or D companies and others were to be stretcher bearers. When he had finished speaking he called to some shadowy figures who were standing nearby and the men were led off after I wished them good luck, to their defensive positions or to the R.A.P. (Regimental Aid Post). It was the last time that I saw them. Johnny Owens took me along in the dark and the stench of the dead grew steadily worse. Johnny explained to me that there were dead Japanese everywhere and we didn't touch them as the Japs came out at night and put grenades under the bodies as booby traps. He then said no more talking, and we walked in silence for about 150 yards. He then grabbed my arm and put my hand on sandbags and I followed him until we turned into a small bunker which had a candle alight and my company commander Jimmy Evans was sitting there dealing with some paper work. He greeted me with "Hello John. Sorry I haven't a chair for you." There was no need for an introduction as I had played rugby football with Jimmy for a couple of years.

I had not been there for half-an-hour when all hell was let loose. There was fire from small arms, mortars and shells which seemed to go on forever. I asked Jimmy if he knew what was happening? And he replied that sometimes it is the result of an attack by the Japs or it could be started by someone who panics on seeing a shadow and all the world starts shooting. Eventually the firing stopped and he said "At first light in the morning we will visit the positions, you will meet the men and I will point out to you where the 'Nips' are. In the meantime, try and get some rest."

Before first light we were given mugs of tea by Roberts my batman and Williams who looked after Jimmy and also looked after the radio. The radio/wireless operator had caught malaria and was in hospital at Dimapur. With the tea came hard tack biscuits with jam on them. To eat, it was necessary to have two people working together, one kept the flies away whilst the other ate and vice versa. You had to close your mind to where the flies had been before you tackled the biscuits.

Just as dawn started to show itself the order to "Stand to" was passed around and the men were put on alert. Jimmy and I moved around from post to post with heads well down because of snipers, and met the men. Most of them were dirty and unshaven and hard to recognise under a camouflaged steel helmet. Many of these men were boys of eighteen or nineteen year old reinforcements which I had brought back from Dunkirk. They had seen service in the Arakan, they had fought their way from Jotsoma to Kohima. They were battle hardened and hated the Japanese, not for what they were, but for what they had done, bayoneted the wounded in the Arakan and had used swords on women and babies in the villages. They also took women and girls from the town they had pillaged as "comfort women".

Just after stand down the shelling started from the Naga village, and we thought that this would be followed by an attack. Jimmy told me that the day before I arrived there had been hand-to-hand fighting going on and the Japanese had lost a large number of men. The proof lay in front of the sandbags, covered in flies.

In the middle of the morning we had a wireless message from the C.O. Lt. Col. Braithwaite to the effect that 'C' Company were coming through us to attack the Japanese positions on Kuki Piquet, which we were facing. The attack was to be proceeded by heavy mortar and shell fire and the troops would now move in under a smoke screen at 2.30 p.m. The plan was changed during the morning for some reason and then changed to

4.00 p.m. The bombardment started about 3.45, just before it lifted smoke was put down on the target and 'C' Company went on up the hill.

There was a great deal of firing and the sound of grenades exploding and in about twenty minutes we had a signal from Major Philip Carrington the 'C' Company commander that they had taken their objectives and would we please stop our men firing as it was shooting his men in the back. I replied that we were not firing, the firing was coming from Japanese that were dug in near trees and branches on the ground and facing the same way as the attack and that I would deal with it.

I very quickly organised a section carrying grenades which they dropped into the fox holes behind the trees. In that attack Philip was wounded slightly, a bullet had pierced the side of his head near an eye and it had come out behind the eye without him losing his sight. He had been wounded in the knee in the Arakan. About half-an-hour later I had a message from Philip telling me that he was sending someone back for a box of 303 ammunition. From out of the smoke there came a tall figure who said he had come for ammo. I looked at him and said "What is your name?" He replied "Baker, sir." I said "You are Bobby Baker and you live in Brighty Avenue in a village called Pontllanfraith, in Brynteg in Monmouthshire." He said "Yes, sir. How did you know?" I took my helmet off and said "Do you remember me Bobby?" He said "Good Lord, John Bennett." We had played cops-and-robbers together when we were children. Bobby went back to Kuki Piquet with his box of ammunition and was rewarded later with the M.M. (Military Medal).

The attacks went on and they were coming in waves. The attack started with mortars and shelling followed by the first wave. They signalled their attack as they moved forward by shouting Banzai and sometimes remarks like "Don't shoot, we are Royal Scots." These attacks were a daily recurrence and there were times when they got into our forward positions and were killed there. We were so close that when the air drops came sometimes they received some of them and occasionally one became caught up in the branches of a tree which remained in no-man's land. At night they used grenade launchers as they were just too far from us to throw them. The spring on the launcher was put under tension and the grenade in a cup, when the trigger released the spring, this threw the grenade about 25 to 30 yards. However, as the spring was released it made a noise like "poing" and which gave us a signal that a grenade was on the way.

One evening it was dark and I left the bunker where the wireless was and went out for a breather and was looking at the stars, when I heard the "poing". I didn't have my steel helmet on and the grenade exploded on the parapet about eight yards away, and something whether it was a small piece of shrapnel or a stone nicked a piece of my right eyebrow which bled profusely. Roberts put a dressing patch on it to keep the flies away and it gradually healed itself.

Some days later after a series of Japanese attacks, I had a very bad headache and felt dreadful. I mentioned this to Jimmy Evans and he said you had better go and see the M.O. and tree dodge your way up. I moved from tree to tree up the hill and eventually came to the R.A.P. where the doctor was working on wounded men. I told him that I didn't feel very well and he asked an orderly to

put a thermometer in my mouth. He took the
thermometer out of my mouth and read it, and said to the
orderly "Put a blanket down for this officer to rest for a
while."

CHAPTER NINE

Returning Home

I thought I had died because when I tried to open my eyes I could see faint figures dressed in white, then a voice said "You have decided to rejoin us again?" I said "Where am I?" The answer was "In a field hospital in Dimapur. We have been pumping quinine into you for about five days. You have had malaria." I can't remember being put in an ambulance or in a bed.

Some days later I had shaved, bathed and been issued with clean clothing and was waiting to return to my unit. Instead I was told to report to an officer where I was told that I had a heart murmur and very high blood pressure and was to report to Poona Hospital. I cannot remember how I did it, but caught a train from Calcutta and ended up in Poona Hospital with a letter from the Field Hospital.

Soon after I arrived there I was given Narcosis therapy for about a week which meant sleep and more sleep, but still my blood pressure would not go down. I had lost a lot of weight too. My normal weight was 10 St. 2 lbs. And I was just 8 St. 9 lbs. My main problem now appeared to be high blood pressure, which was being treated but refused to go down. I was then put on a heart machine and was told that I had Mitral Stenosis, aggravated by malaria, and it was recommended that I be transferred to hospital in Bombay to wait for a boat to the U.K.

Whilst there, I bought a large trunk which I filled with items it was not possible to buy in England, particularly materials, silk etc. Which could be made into dresses for my wife-to-be Margaret, and my sister Beryl. In the bed next to me was a Catholic priest named Timothy Coakley, his home town was Swansea. He had been wounded by a bullet which had scored his skull. He had been padre to a Welsh regiment in the Arakan, and had been lucky to have escaped as his H.Q. had been overrun and the Japanese must have thought he was dead and left him. The position was counterattacked and cleared of Japs and they found Timothy unconscious. He too was waiting for a boat.

Towards the middle of June, 1944 we left Bombay in "The Almanzora" hospital ship bound for "Blighty". When on the journey to the Far East, there was not a light shown on the massive convoy we were in. "The Almanzora" travelled in the night like a well-lit Christmas tree with the red crosses on a white background plain to be seen for miles. We were one of the first boats to go through the Suez Canal which had reopened when North African and Italy had been cleared of Germans. I shared a cabin with Timothy but that was about all. He would, some early mornings, put on his priests attire, and disappear to take a service with some of the crew and passengers. A hospital ship is a "dry" ship, which means no booze for it's passengers, except, in this case Timothy. He would return from his service with a bottle of whiskey, which he kept to himelf.

We were on deck one day when I asked him where he was going when he was finally discharged from hospital. He replied that he had a lady friend in Swansea, who was going to put him up, and added that she had written to him frequently whilst he had been away.

By the time we arrived at Malta I was chess champion of the Officer's Lounge. There were about fifteen of us, Army, Navy and Airforce men. A naval officer boarded the ship at Malta. He sat in the lounge one day when we were heading for Gibraltar watching a game I was playing with another Army chap, which I won. He said "Would you like another game?" and I said yes, and within minutes he had beaten me with his pawns. That was when I relinquished the crown.

I was looking forward to our next stop which was "Gib". I had heard many stories of The Rock and the Barbary Apes that lived on the rock, and of the many tunnels that were bored through it which held stores of food and munitions. Unfortunately just after we left Malta I had a relapse of malaria, and the next time I woke up we were somewhere in the Atlantic. I still haven't seen "Gib".

A week or so later we arrived at the port of Greenock in Scotland where we docked and transferred to a hospital train which was halted in the siding at the dockside. There were normal coaches on the train and coaches which had in-built stretchers. When the moves from ship to train were completed an engine came along which was hitched to the train and we were taken into the main station. There, the good old "Sally Army" people came along with sandwiches and tea, also with paper, envelope and stubby pencil so that we could write home to let them know where we were.

Later on a member of the railway staff came along and unlocked the buffet door nearby. One of the chaps called out to him and asked "Do you have any beer then?" The answer was in the affirmative and in seconds the place was full of men ordering and toasting the first taste of English beer for three years. Beer was also taken into the carriages where the stretcher cases were. This created problems later on when the chaps on the stretchers needed to use the toilet. It was a very peaceful and quiet train that went off into the unknown.

We arrived in Birmingham the next day and were distributed to hospitals in the city. There were about ten officers in the ward I was in, some recovering from wounds, some from malaria and other diseases. There were two officers from another battalion of the R. W. Fus. Who had been bombed by our own planes at Caen and had been cut off for two or three days before they were recovered. After I had been there for about three hours I discovered that under a number of beds were crates of beer which were replaced by the local brewery when empty. It was very pleasant to sit out on the lawns which surrounded the hospital with a glass of beer and for a short while forget about the war.

We were able to write to our loved ones with the knowledge that the letter would reach them in a couple of days and not weeks or even months, and to receive letters that had been written about two days before receiving them. It reminded me of the time in Kohima when we were being attacked by day and night and mail arrived by air drop. One of my men came to me and showed me a letter he had received from his wife telling him that she was leaving him and taking the baby to live with another man. It was one time in my life I didn't know what to do, or say.

Since leaving Bombay I had put on a stone in weight, but my blood pressure was still very high. I had to ration myself to two bottles of beer as more than that affected my breathing and my face and chest became very flushed. After ten days in hospital I was given a lengthy leave and went home to Pontllanfraith. Beryl my sister had been married to Roy (Cutts) on 29th April, 1944. He was a lieutenant in the Provost Corps (Military Police) and was due to go abroad quite soon. We had spent a little time together when he came home on a short leave, and I gave him my Sam Brown belt. He eventually ended up in India. Beryl, Margaret and her sister had all left college and were in their first jobs, Beryl in Maesy Cwmmer, which was near home, Margaret in Ilford and Trissie (Beatrice) in Oakdale near her home. All three were home for the school summer holiday and as Margaret and I had planned our wedding for 23rd August, 1944, there were many activities in preparation of the wedding going on.

My brother Roy was somewhere in Egypt and was due for leave quite soon. Both my parents were out at work, Mother as district nurse, Dad accounts department local council offices by day, wireless, signals Home Guard by night. Margaret's father, John Evans (Pop) was under-manager of Oakdale Colliery, and local magistrate. His wife, Margaret's mother, died in childbirth and his eldest daughter Lena had brought all the children up. She had been through all the trials of bringing up the family, but had none of the pleasure or happiness and comfort that a normal marriage would have given her. Pop had three other children in the family. Clifford the elder child worked in the mine, Douglas in the Navy and Joan in university. Clifford was married, and living in Wyllie near Pontllanfraith.

On 23rd August, 1944 Margaret and I were married in the Weslean Church in Pontllanfraith, and spent our honeymoon at Cwmcarvon Court near Monmouth. It was a large country house with orchards around and belonged to Kenneth Spence the man that Joan had recently married. It was an ideal place to relax in, and for a while to forget about the world conflict. After our honeymoon we both returned to Ilford as I was still on leave. Trissie had applied for and obtained a teaching post in Ilford and managed to get a room in the same house that Margaret and I were in.

Both day and night we were bombarded by flying bombs (Doodle Bugs) and rockets, and often when the sirens sounded Trissie would not leave her bed to go to the bomb shelter. At first it worried both Margaret and me, but when we saw the immense holes and devastation the rockets made when they exploded we understood her thinking. It was a question of where you are, or were, when it landed.

In November, 1944 Margaret announced that she was pregnant, as a result of this I went to see her Education Officer who very kindly accepted her resignation and allowed her to leave immediately. We spent Christmas at home together. On the way home from Ilford to South Wales Trissie travelled on the train with a young Flight Lieutenant called Tom Enoch, who was travelling to Tonnau for Christmas. She and Tom became friendly and over the Christmas period Tom was invited to Oakdale where he was introduced to Pop and Lena, and the rest of the family. Tom was a navigator in a bomber squadron and had recently been shot down by enemy anti-aircraft fire and fortunately had only received minor injuries when the plane crash landed.

Shortly after Christmas Tom and Trissie became engaged and were married on Margaret's birthday 27th June, 1945. At the end of January, 1945 I was posted to Brecon in South Wales. Brecon is up in the mountain, very bleak, and in winter, very cold. I sat by the fire I the Officer's Mess with an overcoat on, and a scarf around my neck, shivering with Malaria. A major came in and said "Do you realise you are sitting in my chair?" I can't remember what I said to him, but it was not very polite. I was back in hospital in the afternoon and in a few days sent on leave again.

My next posting was to a unit described as a holding battalion at Newtown in Mid Wales. I was responsible for ensuring that men who had been discharged from hospital, or arrived from overseas, prisoners of war etc. were given a pass, which was a form of identity card, accrued pay and holiday allowances, and were correctly dressed. Travel documents were made out for them and they were ferried to the bus or railway station. We tried to get the men out within forty-eight hours after arrival. Some days were quiet when only a few reported. Then occasionally fifty would arrive from all over the country. That meant overtime for everyone.

Margaret was staying with me at a private house in town. Some days I could go home and have lunch with her, other days when I was late, the elderly couple who were Welsh speaking and chapel goers would say to her things which would suggest I was up to no good, staying out this late.

In the centre of the camp was an area where there were three large huts enclosed by high wire fences where the A.T.S. women were billeted. They were typists, telephonists, stores personnel and cooks etc. and were a great deal of concern to the C.O. and me as quite often there were holes cut in the wire which would allow men in or women out. Our baby was due in July and in June Margaret decided to go home so that she could make regular visits to the clinic and hospital. I had made arrangement for her to have the baby at a private maternity home in Newport, and a car had been laid on to take her, when the time came.

On the 5th July, 1945 my father rang me to tell me that a boy had been born on the fourth of July. He had rung the couple where Margaret and I had lived in Newtown and told them, thinking I still lived there, but when Margaret left for home I had gone back to the mess, and they had not passed the message on. My C.O. was very understanding and gave me leave for three days so that I might visit Margaret and the boy. As there were difficulties with local transport and restriction on how far buses etc. could go. I did a roundabout journey by train to Shrewsbury and Hereford, and thumbed my way to Newport.

Margaret was very tearful on seeing me, she had felt very much alone having seen very few visitors, and the atmosphere in the home was not good. There were three young mothers in her ward and one had been told that her husband in the R.A.F. had been shot down, and another that her husband had been killed in action. The senior nurse in the maternity home agreed I could take Margaret and the boy home, and my friend the taxi man from Blackwood came and picked us up. We first went to Oakdale so that Pop and Lena could see the baby and then went to 7 Brynteg, to my home. Not long after returning home with John, Margaret left with the boy and went back to Oakdale as Beryl, who was teaching in Maesy Cwmmer caught scarlet fever, which was very contagious.

About a month after John and Margaret went back to Oakdale I applied for a post in the Records Department of the Ordnance Corps in Leicester. I attended a ten-day course and was then put in charge of a department that dealt with "killed", "missing in action" and (P.O.W.) "prisoners of war". My job was to inform the next of kin of the soldiers of their loss. To send telegrams and letters of condolence and to answer queries sent in to the department.

It was not a pleasant job, but very necessary. The war was coming to an end, and notices were posted in the office where I worked requesting that officers who were interested in working for the army of occupation in Germany should write in and apply for an application form. As at the time I was coming to the end of my thirteenth year of service in the Army, it seemed to me to be a continuation for my career. I wrote in and applied, and was invited to attend for interview at the War Office in London. I was provisionally accepted, then sent to hospital for a physical examination. I was informed some days later that regretfully, I was medically classified in 'C' grade for the following reasons:

- Very high blood pressure
- Mitral Stenosis
- A history of malaria

… and was unable to be considered for the post. I went to see my own M.O. and asked his advice. His advice went like this – 'I think John, that you have had enough.

Resign your commission and apply for a disability pension, and I will support your application.'

I went home for the weekend and discussed the future with Margaret. She was very pleased when I told her I would be leaving the Army, and she also said 'I would not have liked it if we had been posted to Germany and we can now plan for a home of our own.' A short while afterwards I handed in my resignation.

The war in Europe had come to an end, but we were still fighting the Japanese in the Far East. We were overcoming their armies which were being decimated. They were short of food and ammunition and malaria and other diseases were rife. Having spent three years fighting in Burma I knew what the conditions were like and my thoughts were with the men and women who were there. It seemed that the war there would never end. Then on 6th August, 1945 the first nuclear weapon in history was dropped on Hiroshima, followed on 9th August by a second on Nagasaki. Raids on Japanese cities continued until 14th August, when, following the personal intervention of the Japanese emperor Hirohito, the Japanese government accepted the terms of the Allies, which were unconditional surrender. The war with Japan was at an end.

In Burma the British fought their longest land campaign of the war. "British" is, however, an incorrect description because more Indian troops fought in Burma than all of the Allies added together. There were Africans, Chinese, Americans and troops from the Commonwealth.

CHAPTER TEN

Back In 'Civvies'

I was heading towards my discharge from the Army and I had no earthly idea what I was to do. However, when on weekend leave Margaret and I and John were invited out to tea with my brother's fiancée May. During tea time, the question over my future cropped up and we talked about possible work situations. Then May said "Have you thought about teaching?" I hadn't done, but when I recalled my school certificates, and the Army exams that I had taken, we decided that I was sufficiently qualified to apply for teacher training. I then wrote to the Ministry of Education and received an application form from them, which I completed and then sent off. About a week later I was sent an invitation to attend an interview at County Hall in Cardiff.

As I was still in the Army I attended the interview in uniform, Sam Browne and shoes shining. There were two other men who were seen before me, and as they came out I asked how they had got on, and they both said it was OK. My name was called. 'Captain John Bennett.' It sounded very impressive. As I walked into the office there were three gentlemen sitting at the table, and to my delight, the one in the middle was wearing a Royal Welch tie. My regimental tie. I was not asked one question aimed towards a child's education, but many about where I had been, names of some of my brother officers and general questions of the war in Burma. After about half-an-hour I was thanked for attending and told that I would be hearing from the Ministry before

152

Christmas. I did so and was advised that I had been selected for teacher training and would be sent further details in January.

At the end of the year I received a letter from the War Office to tell me that the King had authorised them to grant me the honorary rank of captain and another letter from the Ministry of Education granting me an allowance for me and my family for the duration of my training. That, and my disability allowance, was sufficient for a reasonable living.

I worked hard at my studies, and when possible went home to Margaret and John at the weekends, and the year went very quickly. In December, 1947 I sat the final exams and was awarded my Teacher's Certificate.

My first post was at Georgetown Secondary Modern School, Tredegar, in Monmouthshire, teaching General Studies. The standard in English and Maths was appalling. The children were suffering the affects of the war, lack of teachers and particularly changes of teachers as men were called up for service. This prompted me to become interested in remedial teaching and working with less able children.

My next move was to a Home Office School for Delinquent Boys aged between 14 and 16 years of age, at Boreathon School in Shropshire. By this time our family had increased to two boys, John our first born, and Anthony born in September 1947. We lived in a new three-bedroomed house overlooking a lake, meadows and woods about half-a-mile away, and behind the woods a river. It was an ideal place to bring children up, no traffic and lots of fresh air. The school boys were from Birmingham, Manchester and Liverpool, with a history of delinquency, non-attendance at school, and many of their parents were in prison or working in prostitution. In addition to General Studies I took boys for boxing lessons and became an officer in the school cadet company. It was very demanding work and every three days I was on duty until 10.00 p.m. as the boys had to be supervised at all times when in the classroom, or at work outside.

They all had to take part in work situations, gardening, animal husbandry, forestry, kitchen and dining room, cleaning and polishing, painting and decorating. All staff took part in supervision in teams of three. Sometimes a boy would run away (abscond) and make for the nearby railway. If he walked north along the line, he would, after ten miles or so, reach Oswestry, where the police would be waiting, and he would be returned to school and receive the cane. The same thing happened if he went south to Shrewsbury. This did not happen often.

In 1951 Elizabeth was born at home on 16th September. The day before her birth I went to the wood and shot a brace of pigeons. These I casseroled and after she was born and in her cot, I served casseroled pigeon to Margaret and the district nurse who had supervised the arrival. As an endearment, she (Elizabeth) was called "Pigeon".

When John was ten years of age he passed the elven plus examination, and was due to start secondary education the following year, which meant that he would have to travel each day either to Shrewsbury or Oswestry, which in our opinion was too far for a ten-year-old. Anthony was now eight years old and

Elizabeth four. Margaret and I decided that we would apply for posts which were a promotion for me and which were also central for the children's schooling.

Harlow, in Essex was rather more a large village than a town. The area had been chosen as the site for development to take in large numbers of families from the east end of London, which had suffered so badly from bombing during the war. An industrial area was planned and built first, and as the housing became available families were moved in. I was attracted to this new venture as there were chances of promotion within my own special field, and there was living accommodation too. I applied for the post of Head of the Remedial Department at Mark Hall School in Harlow. It was a comprehensive school planned for 1200 children. I was invited to attend for interview and was appointed to start in September 1955.

My work entailed rather more than running a remedial department, as the children I had to admit would, under normal circumstances have been in a school for handicapped children i.e. a special school. I had a small number of children for whom English was a foreign language, epileptics, spastic children, speech defective children and generally backward children. I was allotted four classrooms and I appointed three other teachers experienced in remedial work. My wife Margaret was one of them. In September John was admitted to Nettleswell Grammar School, Anthony to Purford Green Junior School and Elizabeth started kindergarten.

After one term with my department Margaret applied for the post of Deputy Head of Purford Green Junior School and was appointed to the post. In later years both

Anthony and Elizabeth were taught by Margaret for a year.

A couple of years later, because of my knowledge of intelligence tests and testing also maths and reading tests, I was given the job of visiting the junior schools in the catchment area for Mark Hall during June and July of each year, and arranging for each child to be admitted to a group of like ability. There were eight groups with approximately thirty children in each group. Towards the end of the long summer holiday, all the new children who were coming to school in September were invited to school to meet their teachers, to see their classroom and where they would sit. As a result there was no confusion on the admittance day and all went like clockwork.

When I had been teaching in the Mark Hall School for about seven years I applied to the local authority for a sabbatical year so that I could take a diploma course at the University of London Education Department. It was granted and I commenced the course in September 1962. There were weekly lectures on child development, and I, like the other students, visited establishments for people with mental defects and worked in different departments of the institutions, schools for the deaf and blind, physically handicapped and cerebral palsied units. It was a very comprehensive course and I enjoyed every minute of it. There were two morning-long written exams at the end of the course, and the day afterwards when it had finished my brain was numb. However, the following day I was presented with my diploma, which was the first step in my promotional ladder.

Shortly after we moved to Harlow I registered my family with a Doctor Head, a very pleasant fellow who like us had recently moved to the town. One holiday from school Anthony complained of not feeling very well and when we looked at him carefully, found that his eyes were jaundiced. Margaret rang Dr. Head after breakfast, and assuming the doctor would come after surgery Anthony got into bed with me. We were very cosy and warm together when the doctor arrived without warning and caught us in bed. We all had a laugh about it. Anthony was put on a special diet and soon got better.

Later, the doctor asked me whether I would be interested in forming a community association, with a group which included one of his colleagues, two shopkeepers and two other local people. We formed a committee and I was appointed chairman. Within a year just about every householder in Nicholls Field area was a member and representatives were appointed to the roads, they collected subscriptions and marked up the cards of the members. With the money collected and other grants we were able to start planning for a community hall. The Development Association were very kind and their representative on our association committee arranged that we were given a plot of land, and that their architects and surveyors made the plans for the initial building which could be added to as the funds were raised.

Eventually we had a building which was used for Whist Drives and dances and other functions. Harlow was being developed quite quickly and it was announced that quite soon we were to receive a visit from the Queen and Prince Philip. A few weeks before their visit I received a letter inviting Margaret and myself to meet them, and to lunch afterwards. I had to ask my head teacher for time off to attend the function which he, Mr. Gerald Palmer, gave me the day off, and then said "I'll see you there John." He had also received an invitation.

In 1964 we had been in Harlow nine years. John had commenced his studies at London University, Anthony was about to move into 6th Form and Elizabeth was just finishing her first year at Mark Hall. Essex County Council Education Department were building two special schools. One in Chelmsford, called The Hayward School, the other in Harlow, The Commonside School. I applied for the headship of both schools, and after an interview was appointed to The Hayward School to commence September 1964.

From September Margaret was appointed deputy head of King's Road Junior School Chelmsford. Anthony was given a place at King Edward School for Boys and Elizabeth a place at Chelmsford County High School for Girls, and as our new home in Chelmsford was not ready, we travelled from Harlow to Chelmsford and back daily until Christmas time. Just before Christmas 1964 we moved into our new home.

The years seemed to fly by, and at one time, we thought the children would never leave home. Suddenly John and his girlfriend decided to marry and the next day left for South Africa, John to teach, Anne to practice her dentistry. Not long afterwards Anthony and Susan were married, they moved to Colchester. Elizabeth finished her dental training, worked briefly in London, and then decided to go to Australia. The nest was empty.

In the following years the head master of King's Road School became ill and Margaret was acting head for about two years. She did not like office work and preferred to be in the classroom. She indicated this to the governors who then appointed a new head. In addition to my work at the Hayward School, I occasionally lectured at the Cambridge Institute of Education on special education, and at the Brentwood Teacher Training Unit on teaching methods with special needs children. I was also chairman of the Essex Special Schools Section of the National Union of Teachers until I retired.

Margaret and I enjoyed life. We often travelled abroad, and often entertained our friends and relatives. There were also sad times when we lost members of our family.

The children were now carving out their own futures, they made mistakes, like we all do at times, but I think profited from them. In 1981 Margaret and I retired. We spent long holidays in Malta, France and Spain, and stayed with Elizabeth and her family in Australia for three months. I enjoyed it, but Margaret became homesick and was glad when we returned home. In 1987 we began to feel that it was time to move from our home of twenty-three years. The lawns and gardens needed a lot of attention and as the children had gone the home was too large for us. With John's help (at that time he lived in Great Dunmow) we moved to Godfrey Way, quite near John. It was a modern flat with two bedrooms and just right for us. One of our neighbours was Peggy Swallow, an ex-teacher at the local comprehensive school. She was chairman of "The Dunmow Flitch Friendship Club", which had been started by two doctors, a husband and wife called Tasker. The club was started to provide entertainment for people over sixty from Dunmow and surrounding villages. The Taskers had retired to Norfolk.

Peggy Swallow invited us to join the club, Margaret on the committee as Catering Officer and myself as Entertainment Officer. My main task was to provide varying entertainment for our members on the second Tuesday of each month from 7.00 p.m. until 9.00 p.m. One outing a month or a pantomime or play. The programme went well for about two years when Peggy Swallow became ill and suddenly died. Exactly a week later Peggy Perry the Secretary of the club died leaving me as Entertainment, Chairman and Secretary, for about a year. On 21st July 1992 I think, in recognition of our services to the community we were invited to Buckingham Palace Garden Party, where again we were presented to the Queen and other members of the Royal Family.

In 1996 Margaret's doctor diagnosed that she was suffering from Parkinson's Disease and also Osteoporosis. Sometimes, without warning, she would fall, but not hurt herself. In the period 1996 – 1999 she had broken both arms and had two hip replacements, and in 1998 was found to have cancer of the colon. This was operated on but her condition worsened and on 20th August, 1999 my sweetheart died, just a few days before our fifty-fifth wedding anniversary. She was a wonderful wife, mother and grandmother, and also my best friend, and I miss her a lot. She was a very special person.

I am now approaching my eighty-eighth year, and in reasonably good health. I have seven grandchildren, all sound in mind and limb, for which I am grateful. When I look back on my life, I can honestly say that I consider myself as a most fortunate man, and I am also extremely proud and pleased with the achievements of my children, John, Anthony and Elizabeth.

Earlier, I told part of a story about my boyhood friend Elwyn Lewis. He like his father who was a vicar, and brother Herbert, who had attended Aberystwyth Ecclesiastical College wished to follow in their footsteps, and when he left school with the necessary qualifications, he applied to attend the same college as Herbert. He was successful and had started his training. Unfortunately, his girlfriend became pregnant and Elwyn was obliged to leave the college. He was then conscripted and as an intelligent person trained as an infantry officer. When his training was completed he was posted to a battalion in the Inniskilling Fusiliers.

At the beginning of 1943 I was in a Daka hospital after being nicked by a Jap bayonet, when an orderly came along with mail from home. Both were from my mother who gave me family news, and then wrote "Keep an eye open for Elwyn Lewis, he is somewhere in India." A bit of a tall order. Five minutes later Elwyn appeared on the veranda where I was sitting. His face, and particularly his eyes, were yellow. Apparently he was on the train being taken down to the railhead and from there to where fighting was going on, when he had jaundice and was sent to hospital. We chatted for a while, then he reported in, and was placed in quarantine. I went to speak to him from the doorway a number of times. Then I was sent on leave to Calcutta. When I reported back to the hospital Elwyn had gone to join his regiment in the Arakan.

Two weeks later I returned to the Arakan and was sent on patrol to the mountainous area which ran down the Mayu Peninsular. Occasionally men of the Inniskilling Regiment in very poor condition, exhausted and without food and water for days were coming in. Their story was, that their commanding officer had commandeered any craft he could to ferry men across the Maya River to make a surprise attack on the Japanese. This was done in half-light before dawn. They were halfway across the river when the Japanese appeared, strafed and sank every boat. There were hundreds of men lost. I learned that Elwyn was amongst them. Elwyn's only child was a girl.

When I arrived home I had a visit from Elwyn's wife and her father requesting news of Elwyn. I could only tell them what I have described here. When the war finished, Herbert, who had been padre of a Welsh regiment in Burma, went home. He became enamoured with Elwyn's widow and eventually married her. They had two daughters. I understand that the three daughters are now married with families of their own.

CHAPTER ELEVEN

Keeping In Touch and Remembering

I served for thirteen years with the 1st Battalion of the Royal Welch Fusiliers, which was part of the 6th Brigade and of the larger unit, the 2nd British Infantry Division, which saw service in Belgium, France, India and Burma in the 1933 – 1945 war.

There were many famous regiments in the 2nd Division, to name but a few, 2nd Battalion Durham Light Infantry, 1st Battalion Royal Berkshires, 1st Battalion Royal Scots. After the war I joined the British Legion, and the Burma Star Association, and went to the reunion in the Albert Hall. But each year, there were fewer attending as old comrades "Fell off the perch."

There was also the 2nd Division Kohima reunion, but with the passing years one was fortunate to meet two or three old comrades.

On 18th July, 2004 my friend David Pickford and I went to the final Kohima reunion which was being held in York. David had been a soldier after the war and was a radar specialist, and interested in military history. On Saturday evening 17th July we attended the officers mess dinner in very exalted company. There were members of the Church Officers in their bright and smart uniforms, and as advised, members of the associations in "black tie". There were also ladies tastefully attired in long dinner dresses. I could see that David was a little apprehensive and over awed by the company. However when we went in for dinner David was sitting between the Chaplain-General of the 2nd Division and a colonel's lady.

I glanced at them occasionally and saw that he was chatting with them as though he had known them all of his life and obviously enjoying himself. It was a very pleasant evening, and I was happy to have met two of my old comrades there.

The next morning David and I went to York Minster where the Veterans including myself, were introduced to The Duke of Edinburgh. The service started about 12.30 p.m. and was conducted by the Assistant Chaplain-General.

The highlight of the service was the address given by the Archbishop of York, Dr David Hope which I commend to my family and friends and to those statesmen who are responsible for the conduct of the Nation.

Address by the Archbishop of York, Dr David Hope
Kohima Commemoration service
York Minster – 18 July 2004

" Greater love has no man than this, that a man lay down his life for his friends" (Jn. 15.13)

The Battle of Kohima which today we commemorate was the most terrible of the Second World War. A Private of the Royal West Kent's wrote – "They came at us on the ridge in hundreds. Sheer manpower pushed us back from one trench to another ten feet behind: we were overrun by manpower, gradually into one small perimeter less than half a mile square. In that perimeter, we stopped the Japanese army. We were told that the 2nd British Division was on the way to save us…we stayed in our foxholes and prayed to God for the 2nd Division to come and get us and thank God they came. Padre Randolf and Colonel Laverty saved India, the Padre through prayer for the strength for us all to hold on".

It was this crucial battle fought against the Japanese in North Burma in April 1944 which the then Supreme Commander in South East Asia, Earl Mountbatten, described as "probably one of the greatest battles in history".

And I don't suppose that anyone here today had even heard of Kohima before those months in 1944. High in the hills it was a truly beautiful place, cool and fresh where the English found respite and recreation as they walked in the woods or played golf or tennis. Awash with exotic flowers – everywhere wild mauve orchids – it could be described as a veritable Garden of Eden. Yet before that April in 1944 was out it had become a hell hole littered with buildings and bodies broken beyond all recognition and everywhere the terrible stench of death. Where once there had been a tennis court today there are one thousand three hundred and eighty seven graves – the graves of brigadiers as well as privates, tank drivers and stretcher-bearers, signalmen, riflemen, captains and corporals names from every part of these islands – truly for our tomorrow they gave their today.

So, true words indeed - *"Greater love has no man than this, that he lays down his life for his friends."*

And self-sacrifice was no more evident than in this battle of Kohima – a name still regretfully little known and recognized among the majority of the public today as it had been then. Yes, certainly we remember Dunkirk, Arnhem, Alamein, the Somme, Verdun and even further back Hastings, Trafalgar, Blenheim, Waterloo, yet Kohima deserves an equal if not more prominent remembrance than even all of these. For there within the one half square mile perimeter was focused both the best and the worst of any battle anywhere – the best – the indomitable spirit of those who were prepared to stick it out in the unimaginable conditions of those fifteen days. It says much about the human spirit characterized by courage, fortitude, resolution, sheer grit and guts that they did not simply throw in the towel and give up and give in. Not so for here were a group of men for whom it has been written "love of country, unimaginable adversity, distaste for enemy and battlefield, distance from home, plus character training and leadership produced not just a victorious army but even today groups of men who like yourselves at their reunions manifest a heartbreaking regard for each other and for the values which kept them upright for so long". Such was the best of that battle. And "the worst" well the worst of any war the sheer brutality, the maiming, the killing, the death and destruction all of which is contrary to that which we believe to be God's will and God's plan for those whom He has created.

This year sees the 60th anniversary of the Battle of Kohima and as I understand it today is to be the final reunion in its present form here in York. No doubt, reunions maybe now – somewhat more informally – will continue into the future and rightly so. For if ever we forget those enduring values which ensured our freedom from oppression and tyranny then we shall all stand condemned. For in these days when all the talk is of rights, of individual choice, of self-fulfilment, self-determination all of which are exercised so often at the expense of others, an occasion such as this recalls and reminds us of those virtues and values which are about duty and discipline, about self-giving and self-sacrifice in the service of others.

For if we are to be a truly responsible and civilized society then we shall not live either by self-interest or self-service but rather in recognizing that we ourselves are one of another – that one person's attitudes, words and actions always have some effect on another – on the whole.

Remember it was the priest John Donne who reminds us "No man is an island entire of itself; every man is part of the continent, a part of the main". You certainly knew and experienced this in those terrible fifteen days – you needed each other – and so do we – regardless of who and what we are, regardless of colour, creed, gender, race – in our towns and villages, in our neighbourhoods and local communities, throughout the land, throughout the world, yes, certainly, respecting the rights and dignity, the worth and well-being of others but recognizing that these can never be achieved without those necessary fundamentals of discipline, duty and self-sacrifice which so wonderfully characterized Kohima and which still remain necessary foundations – the enduring virtues and values for the whole human family in every age and generation.

Finally, recall the words with which I began - the conclusion of that very moving account by an ordinary

Private who had endured the overwhelming terribleness of Kohima – he spoke of the Padre and of prayer – "the prayer for the strength for all of us to hold on". And tat is my prayer this day – for the strength for all of us to hold on to those things about which St Paul writes in his Letter to the Philippians – truth, honour, justice, purity, beauty, graciousness, excellence – these are the things which make for a human and humane society and which enable us all to hold on – to hold on to one another – to hold on to God, the God who in Jesus Christ gave us the supreme sacrifice of the cross and into whose death and dying all our deaths and dyings are drawn so that with, in and through Him we too may come to a joyful resurrection.

Today, once again gives all of us the opportunity to express our admiration to all of you for all that you did and endured for us – that the peoples of the world may continue to live in freedom. We salute your courage and your bravery. We honour your gallantry and heroism and in so doing we continue our fervent desire and prayer for reconciliation, harmony and peace throughout the world.

Return to Kohima

Early in my writing I stated that I had been to hell on a number of occasions but had been fortunate enough to return from it. Times like 18th March 1943 when the Regiment lost 200 men in one day and later at Indin when the Japanese slaughtered mules and men with sword and bayonet.

The worst place was Kohima where at one period it felt like a "no hope" situation and what made things worse was the loss of men I had lived and fought with in peace and war. Again I returned from it but regretted many times that I was unable to see their graves and to pay my respects.

However, under the "Heroes Return" scheme I have recently (2005) been on a visit to India and Kohima accompanied by my daughter. We visited Garrison Hill, Kuki Picquet and the war cemeteries which are set in green and peaceful surroundings overlooking the town of Kohima.

The 2nd Division Memorial stands below the Kohima War Cemetery and bears the following words:

"When you go home, tell them of us and say, for your tomorrow we gave our today."

I am very grateful to the "Heroes Return" scheme for the opportunity to make my last farewell to my friends.

Finally - A Few Photos Of Interest

Map showing the placement of Japanese and Allied forces during the Battle of Kohima, Burma

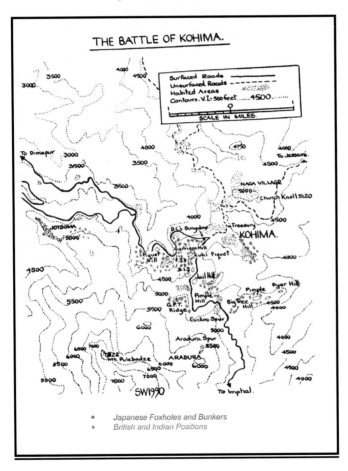

The Author (left), comrade and lifelong friend Doug Lyman (centre) and Jim Cunning,companion traveller to Karachi

The road from Kohima to Imphal showing Garrison Hill in
dense jungle on the Lower Right

British troops in defensive position in action against the
Japanese at Kohima

British defensive position along the Burma Road. There was never peace and quiet for very long, even during hours of darkness.

Arakan 1944 – British troops clearing occupied
Jananese foxholes

Kohima as it stands today. The war cemetery is in the
foreground with the town and former battlefield behind.

The Author revisiting Kohima, scene of action.   Hot,
tired and now a little older than his first visit, he takes a
well-earned rest.

Tommy Radcliffe's memorial stone in the Kohima war cemetery. Sadly I found many others of my fallen friends and comrades there.

4189717 CORPORAL
T. RADCLIFFE, MM.
THE ROYAL WELCH FUSILIERS
5TH MAY 1944 AGE 32

REST IN PEACE

…and these unforgettable and such true words

WHEN YOU GO HOME
TELL THEM OF US AND SAY
FOR YOUR TOMORROW
WE GAVE OUR TODAY

IN MEMORY
OF THE MEN
OF THE
2ND DIVISION

The Duke of Edinburgh meeting some of the Burma Star Association at York Minster in 2004 with the Author just behind to the right

Braided wire blazer badge of the Burma Star Association

A photograph of the Burma Star medal itself which was awarded to all operational British servicemen in the Burma Campaign 11th December 1941 to 2nd September 1945.

*** THE END ***